COACH SELF

[POSITION] **HEAD COACH**
[YEAR] **5TH SEASON**

W-L	%	[OVERALL] W-L
105-29	.784	312-134
HOME	ROAD	NEUTRAL
58-6	25-13	22-10

Full Name: Bill Self
Birthplace: Okmulgee, Oklahoma
High School: Edmond (1981)
College: Oklahome State University
Major: Bachelor's in Business (1985),
Master's in Athletic Administration (1989)

Coaching staff: Kurtis Townsend, Brett Ballard, Danny Manning, Bill Self, Ronnie Chalmers, Joe Dooley, Michael Lee

AN INCREDIBLE YEAR:

KU'S RUN TO THE 2008 NCAA CHAMPIONSHIP TITLE

An Incredible Year: KU's Run to the 2008 NCAA Championship Title
is a joint publication of the *Lawrence Journal-World* and *Sunflower Publishing*
and is Officially Licensed by the University of Kansas

An Incredible Year: 2007-2008 Kansas Jayhawks

ISBN: 0-9742513-6-4

Book published by Sunflower Publishing
609 New Hampshire
Lawrence, KS 66044
www.sunflowerpub.com

Designers: Shelly Kemph, Tamra Rolf
Manager: Bert Hull

LAWRENCE
JOURNAL-WORLD

Book published by Lawrence Journal-World
609 New Hampshire
Lawrence, KS 66044
www.ljworld.com

Editor: Dolph C. Simons Jr.
General Manager: Al Bonner
Managing Editor: Dennis Anderson
Sports Editor: Tom Keegan
Photo Director: Thad Allender

Printing by Jostens, Inc.
4000 SE Adams St.
Topeka, KS 66609

Front cover photograph: Nick Krug
Back cover photograph: Thad Allender

Thad Allender

KANSAS
15

KANSAS
4

NCAA
NATIONAL CHAMPION
KANSAS JAYHAWKS
2008 NCAA MEN'S

CONTENTS

06 Introduction

08 Team Profiles

80 Big XII

92 Big XII Tournament Breakdown

104 NCAA Tournament

112 NCAA Tournament Breakdown

158 Season Statistics

176 Acknowledgements

Nick Krug

INTRODUCTIONS BY GARY BEDORE & TOM KEEGAN

It doesn't seem possible, considering Kansas University's basketball program has been around for 110 years.

But after hearing coach Bill Self say it a handful of times, I now firmly believe it.

We at the Journal-World, kusports.com and Sunflower Broadband Channel Six just finished chronicling, and you the fans, just finished watching - and rooting for - the best basketball team in KU history.

Yes 110 years worth of KU history.

Let's let Self's quote stand as the last words on the matter.

"This is the greatest team in the history of this school and that is unbelievable. It is totally overwhelming," Self said.

Self's Jayhawks, who built a huge 40-12 lead that dwindled to four points en route to a remarkable 84-66 NCAA semifinal victory over North Carolina, then rallied from a nine-point deficit in the last two minutes to trip Memphis, 75-68, in a one-for-the-ages overtime title game, finished the season with a 37-3 record.

The 37 victories were most in school history, two more W's than both the 1985-86 and 1997-98 teams - coached by Hall of Famers Larry Brown and Roy Williams.

Those teams did not win national titles.

Two other KU teams did.

Danny Manning and the Miracles of 1988 were great, but did lose 11 games and didn't catch fire until late.

Phog Allen's 1952 champs, led by Clyde Lovellette, had an '08-like record of 28-3, yet most agree it's tougher to win a national title nowadays with the tournament field set at 64 teams.

Let's not forget giving props to the Helms Foundation title teams of 1921-22 and '22-23, yet Doc Allen's squads didn't have to survive a postseason tourney to cut down the nets in those days.

Self's champs had something in common with so many of KU's legendary teams of the past:

Unselfish play.

Can you believe this KU team had no first-team performers on the Associated Press all-conference team?

That's right?

None.

This team had just four players finish the season as double-digit scorers. Brandon Rush was closest thing to a national "star" with his 13.3 scoring mark.

- Gary Bedore

In late February, to go to the grocery store, the coffee shop, the cigar club, the e-mail box, was to be confronted with the same question, delivered with such angry urgency by friends and strangers alike: "What is wrong with our basketball team?"

After a 20-0 start, coach Bill Self's Kansas Jayhawks had slipped into a 4-3 funk capped off by a road loss to a so-so Oklahoma State team.

Looking back, what was wrong with the Kansas basketball team during that hiccup?

Better question: Who cares?

Answer: Nobody.

The Jayhawks finished 37-3, claiming the national title and completing a 20-year transition from Danny and the Miracles to Mario and the miracle.

It sounds strange to call such a team an underdog, but it actually fit in San Antonio, host city of the first Final Four to feature four No. 1 seeds. Kansas not only was the lone team without an All-American, but also did not have a single player make first-team Associated Press All-Big 12, though guard Mario Chalmers deserved such an honor. Then again, this group wasn't about individual honors, rather it exemplified that in sports sometimes the whole truly is greater than the sum of its parts.

Seven different players led the team in scoring in at least one game. Three were small guards, three were big men, and one, Brandon Rush, was a 6-foot-6 wing, a size distribution that reflected this team's perfect inside-outside balance. An eighth, freshman Cole Aldrich, played national Player of the Year Tyler Hansbrough to a standstill in the first half of a national semifinal.

On this team, players routinely passed up good shots to get better ones for teammates. Defensively, help arrived as a reflex, not an afterthought.

Of course, it was Chalmers who hit the biggest shot in school history, a game-tying three with 2.1 seconds left in regulation, setting the stage for a 75-68 overtime victory against Memphis in the title game, after the Tigers took a nine-point lead with 2:12 left in regulation.

It was Rush who scored 25 points against North Carolina, Sasha Kaun who came up huge in the game before that. Nobody had a better first half of the season than greatly improved Darnell Jackson. Nobody embodied the team-first philosophy more thoroughly than Russell Robinson.

Kansas was a much faster, better team when Sherron Collins took the court healthy, as evidenced by his steal and three-pointer late in the Memphis game. KU was able to get to the national title game without getting a double-figure scoring game from Darrell Arthur in the four games leading up to it, but couldn't have won the school's third NCAA championship without 20 points and 10 rebounds from the sophomore.

Kansas avenged two of its three losses, using 21 points from Rush to defeat Kansas State, and 30 points from Chalmers to defeat Texas in the Big 12 tournament title game. The closest the Jayhawks came to evening the score with Oklahoma State came when Self, three days after winning the national title, turned down his alma mater's offer to return home to coach.

Memorable days and nights lit up the regular season. Players coached by Phog Allen, Dick Harp, Ted Owens, Larry Brown, Roy Williams and Self gathered for a reunion and were honored at half-time of a rout of Colorado. The '88 title team celebrated its 20-year anniversary.

For sheer emotion, Senior Night trumped that reunion. A five-member senior class — devoid of McDonald's All-Americans and flashy games — was long on humility and toughness. The post-game speeches were succinct and poignant, especially those delivered by Jackson and Kaun. Jeremy Case's long-range shooting and overall play during the game floored the crowd.

With Selection Sunday came the revelation that the road to the Final Four wound through Nebraska and Michigan, just as it had in '88, a fine omen. Just as in '88, the Final Four's most outstanding player's father watched from courtside, a member of the coaching staff, Ed Manning then, Ronnie Chalmers this time.

"A combination," Ronnie Chalmers answered when asked if he was a father or a coach when Mario's pivotal three was in the air.

Two three-point shots that seemed forever suspended in the air defined KU's tourney. Davidson's Jason Richards hoisted a buzzer-beater that was wide left. Self watched from his knees and slumped forward, looking more relieved than happy to have reached his first Final Four. Chalmers, with all four living Kansas basketball coaches in the Alamodome, put extra arc on his shot to avoid the outstretched hand of Derrick Rose and drew nothing but net.

In a span of nine days, those two shots and plenty of hard work from Self's selfless athletes ensured the coach would go from carrying the label "best coach never to make it to the Final Four" to the hottest coach in America.

Now, the only relevant question need not be asked: "What's right with the Kansas basketball team?"

The answer is a given: Everything. Life is beautiful.

- Tom Keegan

He is the son of a coach. He played like a coach on the floor. He was born to coach. Yet, somehow, somewhere along the way, Self's reputation became that he could recruit, you better believe he could, but his coaching abilities fell short of his salesmanship. In today's mass-media world, once a reputation takes root, it spreads so swiftly it quickly becomes gospel. It never had an ounce of validity, yet it took reaching the Final Four and winning it for Self to finally get his due. The enduring snapshot will be of him on his knees, the picture of stress, falling forward when Davidson's Jason Richards' three-pointer went wide left. »

Nick Krug

SELF KNOWS HIS STUFF

MARCH 23, 2008 / BY GARY BEDORE

OMAHA, NEB. — ONE WEEK FROM TODAY, IN THE EVENT KANSAS FIFTH-YEAR BASKETBALL COACH BILL SELF TAKES SCISSORS TO NYLON IN DETROIT AND MOVES ONTO HIS FIRST FINAL FOUR, MUCH WILL BE MADE OF HIM BREAKING INTO THE RANKS OF ELITE COACHES FOR FINALLY GETTING PAST THE ELITE EIGHT.

His players, peers and bosses would know that to be so much nonsense. They know that after KU won a grinder Saturday night against UNLV, 75-56, he is one victory away from making his fifth Elite Eight appearance with his third different program, and his third appearance with Kansas. They also know that most college coaches don't ever make it as far as the Sweet 16. They know Kansas could not have a better man at the helm if it had first pick from the other 339 Division I head coaches.

Reaching the Elite Eight is not the goal, of course, but his history of doing it so often does speak to how ideally suited he is to coaching big-time college basketball. His players spoke from the heart on that topic after pushing KU's winning streak to nine games.

"I definitely think he's the best college coach in America, the plays he draws up and just the way he is," junior Brandon Rush said. "He can be a comedian when he wants to, and he's a great communicator. He makes what he's trying to do pretty straight and simple to us."

The public sees the smiling Self, snapping off quick one-liners to take control of conversations. The players, behind closed doors during practice sessions, see all sides.

"When we're playing bad, it's really hard to play for him," Rush said. "When we're playing well, I don't know, he's friendly and funny all the time. He makes you want to play well."

Kansas wasn't playing well in the first half against Lon Kruger's Runnin' Rebels. Senior Darnell Jackson got tied up for a jump ball, and the possession arrow pointed the way of UNLV. Self, using an in-game voice that carries like a Gary Woodland tee shot, let Jackson have it.

"D.J., will you get yourself open!" Self hollered, disgust dripping off of every syllable.

"When he gets on me, sometimes I think he's wrong, but coach Self is always right," Jackson said afterward. "He knows the game. He's been in the game too long."

Of more importance, Self knows people, knows how to get the best out of them even when they are in the midst of personal tragedies, knows how to get them to work as one, even though so many of them arrived at his program as the undisputed center of the universe, their entourages told them so.

Self's .812 winning percentage ranks first among Kansas coaches who coached more than one game. (Karl Schlademan went 1-0 in 1920.) His NCAA Tourney record stands at 8-4. Players don't keep track of such things. They feel themselves becoming better basketball players under him. That's what makes them listen to him, no matter the tone.

"The first time I met coach Self, I just knew there was something about him," Jackson said. "I couldn't figure it out when I first got here. When he kept staying on me so hard, kept pushing me so hard, I understood that he was trying to get the player that was in me out of me. I couldn't understand that, and now I do understand that. I understand that I have to be responsible when I'm on the court and when I'm off the court. Coach Self, man, he's just a great coach, he's a great father, he's a great person, and he's a great friend. That's why every day I see coach Self, I just smile because he's the father figure in my life that I want to be like when I grow up."

Self brings such loose charm to any situation that it's sometimes lost on people how controlling an individual he really is. That quality can make it difficult for him to let up on the reins. Self revealed after the victory against UNLV that before the game one of his former managers sent him a simple message: "Make sure you trust your players."

"I'm getting where I trust them more and more," Self said.

Kansas has such a flexible roster that it's a stretch to say any team presents a bad matchup for the Jayhawks (33-3). That's why they have a legitimate shot to go all the way to their first national title in 20 years. Credit the old point guard's vision for knowing what parts to put together.

"It would be a great accomplishment if we did win that national championship," Jackson said.

Then he smiled, picturing something, but what? What was he picturing? Might as well ask.

"I would love to see coach Self cry," Jackson said. "I want to see some tears come out of his eyes." KU

clockwise from top left: Thad Allender, Nick Krug, Nick Krug, Thad Allender

BRANDON RUSH

[AKA] **B RUSH**
[POSITION] **GUARD**
[YEAR] **JUNIOR**
[NUMBER] **25**

HEIGHT	WEIGHT	PTS
6' 6"	210	507
FG %	3PT %	FT %
.435	.419	.779
PPG	ASSISTS	STEALS
13.3	81	32

Full Name: Brandon Leray Rush
Birthplace: Kansas City, Missouri
Hometown: Kansas City, Missouri
High School: Mount Zion [N.C.] Academy
Major: Communication Studies

Think back to his first Late Night. He soared so high and flashed a shot so pure, yet it looked as if he never had played a possession of defense in his life. Then think about his first night back from ACL surgery. He tried so hard and knew what he was supposed to do, but his body wouldn't cooperate. He was starting from scratch physically. As the season progressed, Rush's physical gifts returned, and at the paint-blistering urging of his coach, he became an aggressive force capable of scoring in bunches, pulling rebounds out of the sky, and shutting down hot shooters. »

Thad Allender

"I think I'm pretty much the exact same guy I was last year, being able to attack the rim, being able to jump like I used to."

RUSH'S POPULARITY HAS CAUGHT UP TO HIS PRODUCTIVITY

MARCH 30, 2008 / BY TOM KEEGAN

UNDERSTANDABLE SUSPICION GREETED BRANDON RUSH IN HIS FIRST DAYS AS A STUDENT-ATHLETE AT KANSAS UNIVERSITY.

For one thing, there was the issue of his tangled high school transcripts. He had been to so many schools, including one that folded and another known more for X's and O's than ABC's. The NCAA Clearinghouse was having trouble making sense of it all. The agonizing drama of waiting to hear word on Rush's status dragged into the school year.

And then there was the issue of his last name. JaRon Rush didn't win any points by referring to former KU coach Roy Williams as "Roy," in a quote in which the player questioned the coach's style. Williams dropped him as a recruit. Strike 1.

Kareem Rush had starred at Missouri, of all places. Strike 2.

Fears arose that because Rush spent a year at Mount Zion Academy in North Carolina — a classic roll-out-the-ball program — he never would buy into the team concept, never would play a lick of defense. He quickly dispelled such fears and was eager to improve. Still, Rush's popularity lagged behind his productivity because the fear he would be a one-and-done player lingered. In the locker room after the loss to Bradley, Rush said he would return. But for how long? One more year. After his sophomore season, he declared for the NBA Draft without hiring an agent and was projected to be taken late in the first round. Then his knee gave out during a pickup basketball game.

"I thought it was a bad knee sprain or something like that," Rush said. "I went to the ground and popped right back up, ran right back on the court and started playing a little bit more. Then it started swelling up real big. When they told me it was an ACL, I was like, 'Why me? Why did this happen to me, especially at this time?'"

He'll re-enter the draft this year. His coach, Bill Self, indicated as much during the Big 12 tournament, saying he was leaving last year so there's no reason to believe he won't this year. It's no longer an issue.

Asked if he expects to go in about the same spot in the draft as he was projected a year ago, Rush started to answer by saying, "I hope ... "

Then he caught himself and said, "I don't know. I really don't know."

Then he smiled and said, "You tried to catch me there."

He'll go to the NBA with everybody's blessings. He worked hard to bring his knee back to life.

"I think I'm pretty much the exact same guy I was last year, being able to attack the rim, being able to jump like I used to," he said. "One thing I'm lacking right now is the lateral movement on the defensive end. I still don't have that back yet." KU

Thad Allender

NCAA
FINAL FOUR
1988
NCAA
FINAL FOUR
1971
6 NEWS
KANSAS

KANSAS
25
13
Preferred
Health Systems
ING

25
MEMPHIS
5

BACK & BETTER THAN EVER?

BRANDON RUSH'S KNEE INJURY MIGHT HAVE BEEN A BLESSING IN DISGUISE. JUST ASK HIS MOM.

FEBRUARY 8, 2008 / BY GARY BEDORE

BRANDON RUSH STILL REMEMBERS THE WORDS OF HIS MOTHER, GLENDA, WHO OFFERED A PEP TALK TO THE KANSAS UNIVERSITY BASKETBALL PLAYER LAST JUNE — A COUPLE OF WEEKS AFTER SURGERY ON HIS RIGHT ANTERIOR CRUCIATE LIGAMENT.

"Blessing in disguise ... that's what my mama said. This might be a blessing in disguise," Rush said before Thursday's practice at Horejsi Center. "My mom always knows what she's talking about, especially about basketball."

The 6-foot-6 junior from Kansas City, Mo., will not go so far as to say he's happy he tore a knee and faced long months of rehab from June 1 surgery.

But, in looking at the big picture, yes, he might be a better basketball player today than a year ago because of all the work he put in while recovering from the surgery.

"I'd have to say overall I'm better," Rush said. "Passing the ball, making shots, getting to the hole. I feel I'm a better player."

And maybe a better NBA prospect.

"Just because of the type of team we've got, balanced, going through the postseason, how far we go there, that will help me out a lot, too. It's possible I could be a better draft pick than I was last year," said Rush, who a year ago was considered a likely late-first-round selection.

KU coach Bill Self says if Rush continues to blossom the rest of February through March Madness, yes, he's a better pro prospect today than back before the 2007 Draft.

"Surgery ... I wouldn't wish it on anyone," Self said. "But if he continues to progress, his draft status and everything will improve in my opinion, based on this season.

"I said all along the ACL would allow him to become a better basketball player over time. This is where we should see it. As he gets real close to 100 percent, the technique things and things he's done to put himself in this position will now allow him to be a better player because he just won't rely on athletic ability," Self added of Rush, currently listed by NBAdraft.net as No. 29 pick (by Detroit) in the first round.

"He's more disciplined. He's more responsible. He probably approaches the game a little bit differently now," Self said, agreeing that Rush is a better passer than a year ago.

"How about the job he did (defensively) on Matt Lawrence (0-for-6 shooting for Missouri) the other night? When he was guarding Budinger (Chase, Arizona, who scored 27 points versus KU) he wasn't ready to do that. He defended him (Budinger) OK. Now he's becoming a lockdown defender we can put on anybody."

Self said Rush, who has practiced without his right knee brace this week and may discard it for Saturday's 7 p.m. home game against Baylor, has gained confidence week by week.

"We've said this all along, he'll get back to close to 100 percent before conference, and Feb. 1 is when he should really kick it in," Self said. "I think the timing's been right on target. A lot is him being aggressive. A lot is, he feels better about himself physically to put himself in those aggressive positions."

Self said he saw Rush jump off one foot "the first time all year" in last Saturday's victory at Colorado, a game in which Rush had a vicious dunk in transition.

"His explosiveness is close to being back to what it was before he got hurt. In his mind, he thinks it's back," Self said, crediting doctors who along the way, "educated Brandon saying, 'this is how you'll feel when you come back. This is how you'll feel after a month and so on.'"

Rush, who averages 12.6 points and 5.1 rebounds overall, has tallied 15.6 points and 7.0 boards in conference games. A 44 percent shooter overall, he has made 45.9 percent of his shots in league play.

"February is a big month for me to step up. I stepped up pretty big in January, too. Since conference started, I've been playing pretty well," Rush said.

Self would second that notion.

"If you were just going to ask me today, I trust him more than anybody," Self said of Rush's defensive prowess compared with KU's other guards. "That could change next week, (but) he's become as good a defender as we have."

He's also been a leader by example. The Jayhawks have noticed his hard work in coming back from injury.

"He worked hard all summer, all fall to get where he is now," said sophomore Sherron Collins. "Now he's back jumping high. We're throwing him lobs. To me, he's back."

He even has some swagger this season, despite the fact Rush says, "nothing makes me mad, except when I get beat on defense."

"He has aggressiveness. He just doesn't show it," Collins said. "If somebody ticks him off he gets a little look on his face and that's when we know he's ready to go." KU

clockwise from top left: Thad Allender, Thad Allender, Nick Krug, Nick Krug

He never went more than two games in a row without scoring in double figures. And then the NCAA tournament arrived and in the four games leading up to the title game, he had a string of consecutive single-figure scoring outputs. All that meant was he was due to come through in a big way. He did, totaling 20 points and 10 rebounds. Hook shots, face-up jumpers, spin moves, slam dunks, that was Arthur, the player teammates call Shady. Just as important, he played defense with his feet and not his hands in helping Kansas to its third NCAA title. »

Nick Krug

DARRELL ARTHUR

[AKA] **SHADY**
[POSITION] **FORWARD**
[YEAR] **SOPHOMORE**
[NUMBER] **00**

HEIGHT	WEIGHT	PTS
6' 9"	225	510
FG %	3PT %	FT %
.543	.167	.702
PPG	ASSISTS	STEALS
12.8	33	20

Full Name: Darrell Antwonne Arthur
Birthplace: Dallas, Texas
Hometown: Dallas, Texas
High School: South Oak Cliff
Major: Undecided

00
15
MIZZOU
at&t

ARTHUR SHOWS CEILING

JANUARY 6, 2008 / BY TOM KEEGAN

BOSTON — ASK NBA SCOUTS TO NAME THE KANSAS UNIVERSITY PLAYER WHO WILL MAKE THE MOST MONEY IN HIS BASKETBALL CAREER, AND MOST WILL ANSWER DARRELL ARTHUR.

They watch him run the court so swiftly, consistently getting back on defense, which allows the guards to protect the perimeter against three-point shots. They watch Arthur catch the ball reliably. They watch him throw down a one-handed slam as he did in Saturday's 85-60 blowout against Boston College in sold-out Silvio O. Conte Forum. They watch him slide his feet so well for a 6-foot-9 player. They love all those ingredients that project future success.

All of that can make Arthur a frustrating player to watch sometimes. At times, he looks a little unsure of where he should be and what he should be doing. Saturday's game was not one of those times.

The sophomore forward from Dallas contributed 22 points, seven rebounds and two blocked shots.

"I said going into the season I thought he was our most improved player," KU coach Bill Self said. "He hasn't played to the level of what I thought his improvement was, to be real candid with you. He needs to be a guy who can average 16 to 18 for us. Night in and night out, he should be able to generate points, and he hasn't done that consistently. So it was great to see him get off to a good start."

Arthur leads the team with a 13.7 scoring average, ranks second with six rebounds per game and leads the team with 22 blocked shots.

He's a force, but why isn't he more of a consistent force?

"He's our leading scorer," Self said. "If you want to really think about this, everybody sees his ceiling, which is so high. How many did (Nick) Collison and (Drew) Gooden average as sophomores, first part of the season?"

Gooden averaged 15.8 points and 8.4 rebounds as a sophomore, the same year Collison averaged 14 points and 6.7 rebounds.

Self forever preaches to Arthur to try to get easy baskets, which isn't as easy as it sounds.

"A lot of it is he doesn't really understand how to put himself in position to get easy baskets," Self said. "When he starts understanding that, offensive rebounds, put-backs, getting to the line, things like that, he'll get better. ... He's really starting to understand the game."

Arthur had four of KU's 10 dunks and didn't waste time floating on the perimeter, which had been a problem early in the season.

Easy shots are harder to find than low-percentage ones.

"It's kind of hard to get them with all the bigs in there," Arthur said. "When you get a chance to score them, you have to take advantage."

On this afternoon, he didn't rush his inside shots, a common problem for young players.

Asked if Arthur dominates in practice, junior Brandon Rush said, "Does he ever. He takes control of practice. His fade-away's unstoppable. You can't block it."

Of himself, Rush said he still is "85 to 90 percent" recovered from knee surgery, and said he thought Sherron Collins was closer to a full recovery from foot surgery. Projecting physical improvement from those two key players and a continued maturing of Arthur's game, it's easy to see Kansas entering the NCAA Tournament as a No. 1 seed, if not the overall No. 1 seed. KU

Thad Allender

ARTHUR TURNS TIME TO POINTS

FEBRUARY 28, 2008 / BY TOM KEEGAN

AMES, IOWA — BASKETBALL IS NOT WITHOUT ITS MYSTERIES. FOR EXAMPLE, THERE WAS THE BIZARRE 1978 DISAPPEARANCE OF JOHN BRISKER, THE FORMER ABA SUPERSTAR WHO FINISHED HIS CAREER WITH THE SEATTLE SUPERSONICS OF THE NBA.

Brisker reportedly went to Uganda, either as a guest invited by basketball enthusiast Idi Amin Dada or to start an import-export business or to become a mercenary fighting for Amin. From there, the story grows even hazier. Brisker, declared legally dead in 1985, rumor has it either died in combat or did something to upset the mad dictator with a penchant for cannibalism and was eaten by him. One wild theory even suggested that Brisker died at the Jonestown Massacre.

At this point, it's not likely the mystery of John Brisker ever will be solved.

As for the question of how it is that a player so tall and quick as Darrell Arthur could go two games in a row without scoring double figures for Kansas University, well, that doesn't even come close to qualifying as one of basketball's mind-bending mysteries. Quite the opposite.

When Arthur plays a lot, he scores a lot. When he fouls a lot, he sits a lot. There you have it. Not exactly as mysterious as trigonometry.

Arthur played 31 minutes, scored 18 points and had 10 rebounds Wednesday night in an uninspiring 75-64 victory against Iowa State in Hilton Coliseum.

Other than a stronger-than-usual rebounding night, it was an average performance at best for Arthur. It's just that his increased minutes made it seem above-average. He made nine of 18 shots from the field. He hits 53 percent of his shots on the season. He didn't get to the free-throw line at all.

His decision-making was probably slightly above average, considering he came into the night with 17 assists in 27 games and had two in the first half, including one ball he wisely sent back out to the perimeter for Mario Chalmers to turn into three points.

Staying on the floor was Arthur's greatest achievement. In his only three games (ISU, Arizona, Baylor) with at least 30 minutes, Arthur has averaged 20.3 points per game. It's not that KU doesn't have a go-to scorer, it's just that passing it to him half the time goes down in the books as a turnover because the rules dictate that when a player sitting on the bench catches the ball, he can't do anything with it but hand it to the referee.

Nothing sets a better climate for open three-point shots than the sort of relentless transition game KU executed in Wednesday's second half. Few foes have big men who can keep up with KU's giants, so the opposing guards have to go all the way down to protect the goal, and the perimeter is left unguarded. The stronger the opponent, the better the job it will do at retreating, which means Kansas will need to get some threes in its half-court offense. The more teams have to double-down on big men, the way Iowa State did, the more clean the three-point shots looks for KU's guards. Again, it's no mystery the Jayhawks hit seven of 11 three-pointers, as open as the shooters were most of the time.

For much of the night, Arthur guarded 6-foot-7 Wesley Johnson, a three-point shooter who doesn't draw many fouls. Arthur committed four fouls, but spread them out enough that he didn't have to sit out long stretches. If Kansas is going to get anywhere close to reaching its goal, this must become the rule, not the exception. KU

clockwise from top left: Thad Allender, Nick Krug, Thad Allender, Thad Allender

1969
1975
12
0

11

KANSAS
00
EASTERN
45
WASHINGTON
15

SPALDING
33
00
VILLANOVA
1

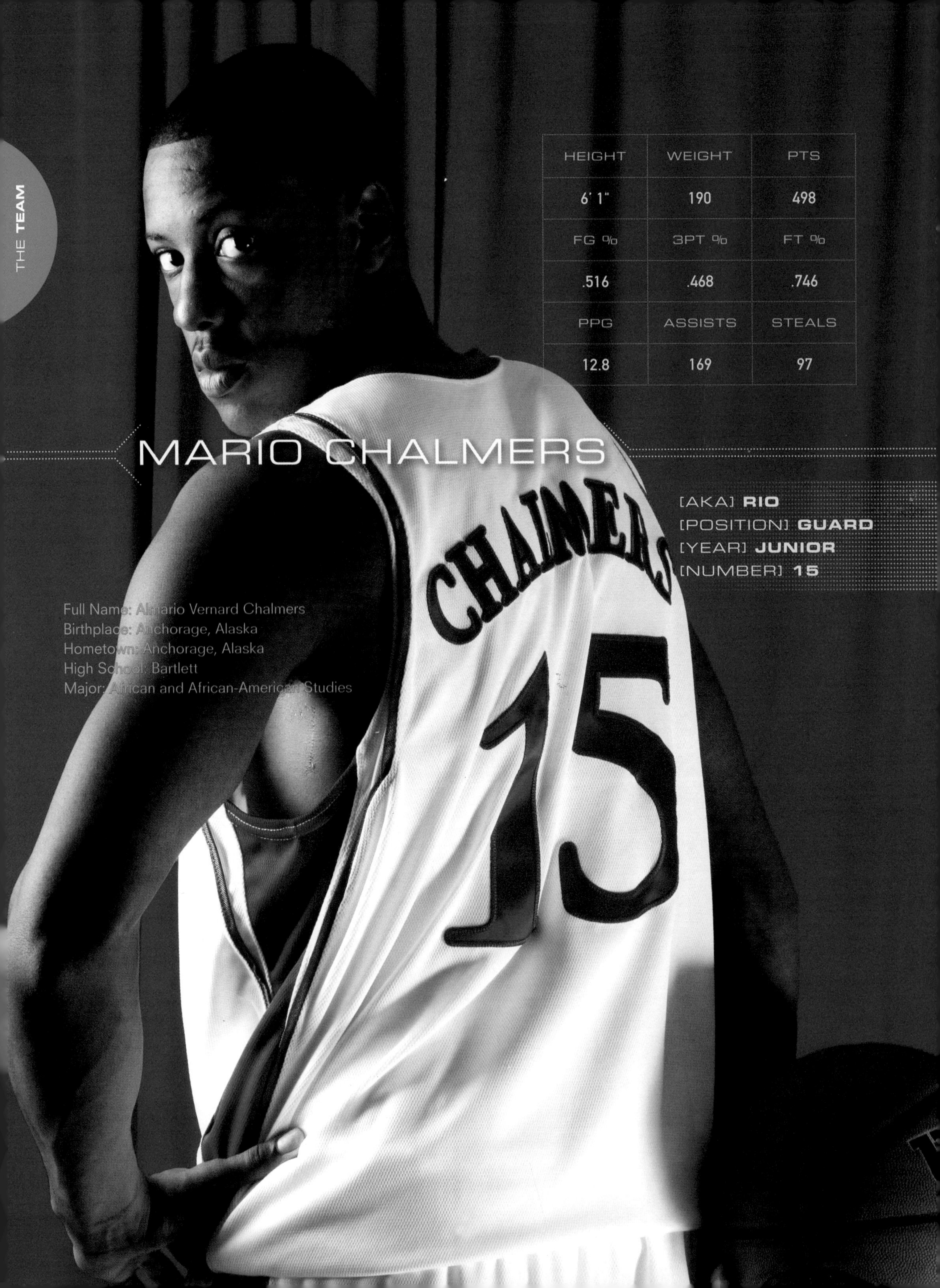

HEIGHT	WEIGHT	PTS
6' 1"	190	498
FG %	3PT %	FT %
.516	.468	.746
PPG	ASSISTS	STEALS
12.8	169	97

MARIO CHALMERS

[AKA] **RIO**
[POSITION] **GUARD**
[YEAR] **JUNIOR**
[NUMBER] **15**

Full Name: Almario Vernard Chalmers
Birthplace: Anchorage, Alaska
Hometown: Anchorage, Alaska
High School: Bartlett
Major: African and African-American Studies

Teammates call him "Rio," but he ought be known as "Big Shot" forevermore. Before hitting the three that made a nine-point lead in the final two minutes vanish and forced the one-sided overtime in the national title game, Chalmers was the team's best player. Name a quality a college guard needs and Chalmers has it in abundance. Whether prowling the passing lanes, pressuring the ball, soaring for a defensive rebound he slaps so loudly, nailing clutch three after clutch three to match Davidson's baby-faced assassin Stephen Curry, he delivered. »

Nick Krug

A THIEF FROM THE START

CHALMERS SHOWED KNACK FOR SWIPING BALLS AT EARLY AGE

JANUARY 12, 2008 / BY GARY BEDORE

LINCOLN, NEB. — SQUATTING IN A DEFENSIVE STANCE WHILE WEARING HIS "GOLDEN GREEN GANG" UNIFORM, MARIO CHALMERS MUST HAVE LOOKED LIKE THE CUTEST, MOST INNOCENT LITTLE 5-YEAR-OLD BASKETBALL PLAYER IN ANCHORAGE, ALASKA, MILITARY LEAGUE HISTORY.

Cute and innocent, that is, until opposing 5-year-olds tried to dribble past him.

"He'd take the other guy's ball," reported Ronnie Chalmers, Mario's dad who coached Kansas University's junior guard in youth leagues as well as at Bartlett High up in the "Land of the Midnight Sun."

"Back in that league, the rule was you couldn't guard until the ball got across halfcourt. He'd be waiting and take it," Ronnie, KU's director of basketball operations, added with a laugh. "He started this in kindergarten. It became a habit."

"This" is the knack of stealing the basketball, something Mario Chalmers does better than anybody in the Big 12 Conference.

Mario Chalmers, KU's 6-foot-1, 190-pound ballhawking guard, who led the conference in steals the past two seasons — recording a KU single-season record 97 thefts a year ago — has a league-best 44 heading into today's 8 p.m. Big 12 opener at Nebraska.

"He's the best I've ever been around at taking somebody else's ball," KU coach Bill Self said of Mario Chalmers, who ranks fourth in school history with 230 steals — combining to form a dynamic defensive duo with senior Russell Robinson, who is fifth in school history with 206 thefts and second in the league this year with 38.

How did Mario become such a standout steal artist?

"YMCA, AAU, high school I used to tell him to count the dribbles. 'Go 1, 2, 3, and on the third dribble, take it,'" Ronnie Chalmers said. "Most times the guy will make his move on the third dribble. The third dribble was the most crucial. He'd use his instinct and get it."

Mario Chalmers, who says he likes "playing defense more than scoring" credits "anticipation and instinct" for his ability to steal the ball.

"I think it's reading the passing lane, like DB's do," Mario Chalmers said of football defensive backs. "They've got to read where the ball is going, try to get in front of it, try to meet the ball before the opposing player does."

Chalmers played some football back in Alaska.

"Nothing too serious, when I was 10, 11, 12. I always played free safety and corner," Chalmers said.

"I couldn't answer that," he said, asked whether playing football helped him on the court. "It could have helped a bit, but I think that I just see it coming and use instinct to go get the ball."

Chalmers says "50 percent" of the credit for his steals goes to his ballhawking buddy, Robinson.

"Russell puts pressure on the ballhandler. When they try to get rid of it, I try to read the pass," Chalmers explained. "Russell is one of the best defensive guards I've ever seen. Russell is tough, plays great defense. I give him credit all the way."

Robinson — he had eight steals, one off the school record, in KU's recent rout of Yale — agreed the two work well together.

"I may help by pressuring the ball," Robinson said. "It makes Mario's job easier. He's so solid. He gets everything set up. We feed off him. He gets steals, and it changes momentum for the team."

Robinson admitted Chalmers' defense "can be a little sloppy at times."

In coach Self's words, that means ... "he's so good at it, sometimes he goes for it too much. But he gets a lot of them."

Self said KU's steals are a thing of beauty.

"Russell sets him up a lot. Other players set him up," Self said. "Mario has very quick hands. He has a lot of God-given quickness, great basketball instincts, and he's just good at it, getting many of them off deflections or creating deflections."

Self said he had no idea Chalmers would be even better at stealing the ball than one of his all-time favorite defenders — former Tulsa player Eric Coley, the WAC's all-time steals leader.

"We thought Mario had great instincts as a basketball player, but there's a lot of things you don't know about guys totally when you recruit them," Self said. "Mario's ability to get his hands on balls is something we certainly thought he'd be good at but no idea he'd be this good."

Thad Allender

Self wants no credit for teaching Chalmers the art of stealing.

"I don't know if it's something you teach. You do teach guys to play with their hands defensively," Self said. "Ronnie may have worked with him a lot in high school. The bottom line is you teach guys to be in the right spots. If they are in the right spots, they can take advantage of their instincts."

Chalmers' steals definitely have led to a lot of exciting moments in Allen Fieldhouse the past three years. And some interesting moments at practice.

"Mario and Russell do the same thing they do in games with stealing every pass," senior guard Rodrick Stewart said. "They play the passing lanes so great. Mario is just great at just taking your ball. From last year to this year, he's on a whole other level just taking the ball away from his man and just locking him up. A lot of their steals are contributed to other guys pressuring their man. It's definitely a team thing, but every time it's those guys," Stewart marveled.

"They make it look so easy out there, too. That's what's crazy to me. I'll just be sitting there like, 'Man, I wish I could get something that easy. Those would all be fast-break dunks.'"

Chalmers seems to convert a lot of his steals into breakaway points. Maybe more so than Robinson.

"A lot of Mario's steals are off the ball, interceptions in the passing lanes," Ronnie Chalmers noted. "Over half of Mario's steals seem to result in layups. Russell gets an assist after a lot of his. But they both result in a lot of baskets. Those two are a tandem. They work well together."

So well ... "I think Mario and Russ are the only two guys that I've played with or played against in practice that have the defensive mindset that they're not going to let anybody score on them," senior Darnell Jackson noted.

Their efforts won't be appreciated by Nebraska's fans tonight, if indeed Chalmers and Robinson pluck any steals.

Monday, however, versus Oklahoma on Big Monday in Allen Fieldhouse will be a different story.

"It's a thrill to steal it," Chalmers said. "You know you are going to get an easy basket, and that's going to get the crowd into it."

He should know. He's been doing it a long time. KU

KANSAS
15

TEXAS TECH
5
O'Reilly
AUTO PARTS

MIAMI
22

KANSAS
15

CHALMERS DOESN'T GET HIS DUE

MARCH 19, 2008 / BY TOM KEEGAN

OMAHA, NEB. — JUNIOR GUARD MARIO CHALMERS' IMPROVED ATHLETICISM SINCE HE ARRIVED AT KANSAS UNIVERSITY INSPIRES A LOT OF TALK WHEN HE SOARS SO HIGH, SO QUICKLY TO BLOCK THE SHOT OF AN OPPOSING CENTER AND WHEN HE ELEVATES TO THROW DOWN A ONE-HANDED DUNK.

It's rare for a player to get so much more athletic, especially considering Chalmers was no plodder when he left Anchorage, Alaska, for Lawrence. His explosive plays understandably inspire a lot of chatter and tend to overshadow another area of improvement from him. An accurate long-range shooter as a freshman (.375 from three-point country), and a better one as a sophomore (.404), he has developed into a dead-eye as a junior (.480).

Chalmers played 33 games as a freshman and has played 33 this season, going into Thursday's opening-round rout of Portland State in the Qwest Center. As a freshman, he attempted 144 two-point field goals and made 73 for a .507 percentage. This season, he has made 74 two-point field goals and attempted 132 (.561).

His assists-to-turnover ratio was 1.37 as a freshman and is 2.32 this season. Quietly, except for his 30-point outburst in the Big 12 Conference tournament title game, Chalmers has developed into a remarkably efficient guard. He shoots more frequently and scores more often, creates more opportunities for others and makes better decisions on the break than at any time in his career.

Chalmers needed just a season-high 15 field-goal attempts to score 30 points. On many teams, he would average close to 15 shots a game. For balanced Kansas, Chalmers has reached double figures in shot attempts just eight times.

Chalmers seldom takes a bad shot, and the same can be said for the entire Kansas team. Think about it: When is shot selection ever an issue with this team? For every field goal attempted, Kansas has generated 1.13 points, excluding free throws on three-point plays. Chalmers, scoring 1.276 points per shot, leads the team in that category. Darnell Jackson (1.275) ranks second.

That sort of team shooting efficiency isn't possible without players being put in position to get good shots and without players having the wisdom to avoid pulling the trigger on low-percentage ones. Both qualities speak to discipline, and ultimately, coaching.

Bill Self's teams play a disciplined brand of basketball, but he tends not to get as much credit as other coaches for that because his teams play at a fast pace. For some reason, discipline tends to be equated with walking the ball up the floor, milking the shot clock and winning low-scoring games.

At times during the Big 12 regular season, the Jayhawks sometimes became undisciplined defensively, going for too many steals and reaching for too many fouls. Offensively, though, the Jayhawks (31-3) remained efficient.

Chalmers doesn't get enough credit for playing with discipline, for taking smart shots, for sharing the ball. Who knows why? Maybe it's because he doesn't have a crew-cut and doesn't answer to the overused "overachiever" label. Whatever the reasons, Kansas is fortunate to have him on its side. KU

clockwise from top left: Thad Allender, Nick Krug, Nick Krug, Nick Krug

HEIGHT	WEIGHT	PTS
6' 8"	250	447
FG %	3PT %	FT %
.626	.333	.691
PPG	ASSISTS	STEALS
11.2	43	31

Full Name: Darnell Edred Jackson
Birthplace: Oklahoma City, Oklahoma
Hometown: Oklahoma City, Oklahoma
High School: Midwest City
Major: African and African-American Studies

Emotional pain and back pain couldn't knock the smile off his face. So many so close died tragic deaths. Nearly all his friends from Oklahoma City took the wrong path and wound up behind bars. And there was Jackson, a fan favorite, rising above it all to throw down lobs, to chase down loose balls in the corner, to swish 15-foot jumpers, and most of all to smile in a way that fueled the Fieldhouse. He saved the best work of his career for his senior year and greatly softened the blow of losing Julian Wright. »

Nick Krug

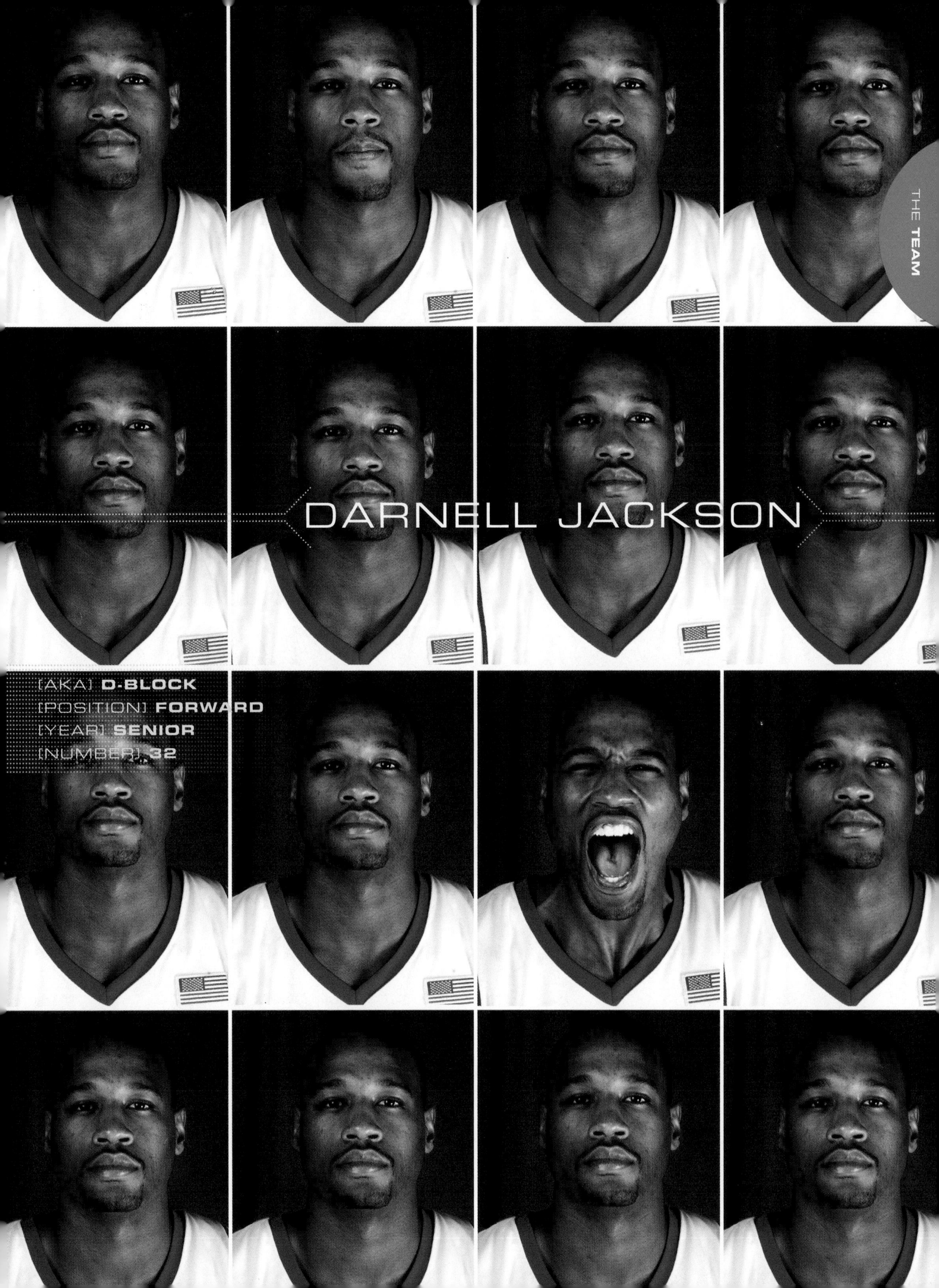
THE TEAM
DARNELL JACKSON
[AKA] D-BLOCK
[POSITION] FORWARD
[YEAR] SENIOR
[NUMBER] 32

NORTH CAROLINA 50
KANSAS 32
NORTH CAROLINA 21

KU

Wilson
ING
O'Reilly

KANSAS 32
O'Reilly

JACKSON HAS CLEAR MIND, BIG IDEAS FOR SENIOR SEASON

FAMILY TRAGEDY IN PAST, FORWARD BECOMES FRONTCOURT FORCE

JANUARY 8, 2008 / BY GARY BEDORE

SHAWN JACKSON, SO STRONG AND BRAVE AROUND HER SON, DARNELL, BEFORE AND AFTER HER 10 SURGERIES THE PAST TWO YEARS, NO LONGER COULD MASK THE PAIN.

Following last July's triple fusion procedure to repair ankle, heel and talus injuries sustained in a May 29, 2005, car crash that claimed the life of her mother, Evon, Shawn confided in her oldest of three children she was hurting ... badly.

"Darnell sat there in the hospital. The doctor's assistant came in and my leg was bleeding. It was horrible. So bad. He saw me crying for the first time since his grandmother's funeral," Shawn said of Darnell Jackson, Kansas University's 6-foot-8, 250-pound senior basketball forward from Midwest City, Okla.

"I said, 'I've been in pain two years, and I can't do it any more.' Darnell said, 'Mom, if you can hold on, I will help you. I will help you,'" Shawn Jackson, victim of a drunk driver who is currently serving 10 years in prison, related.

A strong woman, Shawn did recover from her latest surgery with the support of Darnell's younger siblings — Ebony (18) and Evan (16), who live in her Midwest City, Okla., home — as well as Darnell, who returns to Oklahoma when he can and cell-phones his mom two to three times a day.

"I love talking to her. It helps a lot when she calls and lets me know exactly what is going on," Darnell said of Shawn, who has come to grips with the fact she is "disabled for life."

Shawn looks at the bright side ...

"She tells me I don't have to worry about anything. She's doing great. Knowing that has helped me a lot," Darnell said.

BEHIND THE SMILE

Knowing mom is doing so well two years after both her leg and forearm were shattered in the senseless accident has helped Darnell Jackson fully embrace his final year at KU.

There are times he's still overcome with emotion — like Saturday when he was brought to tears at halftime of a blowout victory at Boston College thinking of his beloved grandmom. More often than not, however, Darnell has been carefree on the court through 14 games of the season.

He not only rejoices after amazing plays like his one-handed catch of a lob and dunk against DePaul and driving spin move for a hoop versus Yale. The big guy smiles and beats his chest after big plays by his teammates, too.

"I enjoy smiling. I know I have a great smile. I get it from my mom," said Darnell, smiling Monday after being named Big 12 co-player of the week with Texas' D.J Augustin as a reward for a career-best 25-point outing against the Eagles.

"When I am out there having fun and smiling, I think it helps my teammates get a little boost of energy so we can play harder for the fans."

Watching Darnell smile makes mom, who attends some home games in person and watches the rest back home on TV, smile.

Her son, who first played organized basketball in ninth grade, has blossomed into a bonafide college standout, a player averaging 12.5 points (second-best mark on team) and team-leading 6.7 rebounds who has started to attract the interest of NBA scouts.

"He's always been happy," Shawn said. "It's just that his first three years were hard because of everything that had happened — him taking everything in and dealing with it on a day-to-day basis."

That includes the death of his dad at the age of 13, as well as deaths of an uncle, cousin and childhood friend the past few years.

Also there was the NCAA-mandated nine-game suspension Jackson's sophomore year as punishment for accepting benefits from a booster, not to mention his persistent back problems.

"He's at the end. He knows he's going to graduate on time. He knows things are good at home. More than anything he loves the game," Shawn Jackson said. "My family ... the couple of games they've seen, they are, 'Oh gosh, he's playing well.' I said, 'You haven't seen anything yet.'"

Shawn figured something special was happening last summer when her son worked out day and night at Oklahoma City University.

"I think practicing with those guys (OKC players) every day gave him confidence. He got it through his head, 'I didn't just come to Kansas to be a role player,'" Shawn said. "I had not seen him play this summer because of my surgery, but I heard he was doing well. Now I'm in awe. I knew he'd gotten better. Seeing him now ... oh my gosh, it's wonderful."

"I worked hard all summer," Darnell said. "I watched some of the moves of 'Shady' (Darrell Arthur) and Sasha (Kaun) and some of the things coach (Danny) Manning told me and practiced moves on my own." »

clockwise from top left: Nick Krug, Nick Krug, Nick Krug, Nick Krug, Thad Allender

FROM SQUARE ONE

The only moves the standout football tight end had on the court when he took up the sport in ninth grade at Oklahoma City's Northwest Classen High School were ones that resulted in turnovers.

"He couldn't play. I won't lie," Shawn said.

Why did he even try?

"I did it because one of my best friends asked me to go out for the team with him," Darnell said. "We made the freshman team. The next day we made the varsity team. I wasn't very good but stuck with it the whole way."

He was supported all the way by Shawn and her brother — Darnell's beloved uncle, Edred, the father figure in his life.

"Darnell didn't have any coordination in basketball," Edred recalled. "He had never played it at all. I think he didn't think he had it. Like most kids ... they want to come out and be Michael Jordan as soon as they touch the ball. I always told him, 'You've got to practice real hard.' He was discouraged he wasn't as good as other kids his age."

A good athlete, Darnell improved quickly at basketball.

He averaged 20 points and 12 rebounds a game his junior season at NW Classen. He moved to Midwest City High his senior year and posted 18 points and 16 boards a game.

Darnell orally committed to KU the summer before his senior year, having also received interest from Oklahoma, Arizona, Illinois, Purdue and New Mexico.

He averaged 2.0 points and 1.7 rebounds while playing sparingly his freshman season, upping the numbers to 6.3 points and 4.9 boards his soph campaign and 5.5 points and 5.1 boards last season before erupting as a senior.

"I am real surprised about it. I never knew I'd get this far playing at the University of Kansas. Everything is coming true," Darnell said.

Not only because of the work he put in last summer, but the fact he's at peace with everything going on around him.

"He's improved a ton," KU coach Bill Self said. "He's a smart player. He grasps things quickly. He's a good shooter, good passer. Look at how many points he scores off hustle plays. His enthusiasm is infectious.

"But the biggest reason he's playing well?" Self asked. "He's playing well because his mind is free. That is the biggest reason."

Self would know. Last year about this time he embraced Darnell at the conclusion of a lengthy meeting in Self's office in which Jackson pondered giving up the sport so he could move home, be with his mom and continue to mourn the loss of his grandmom, whom he refers to as "an angel."

"The hand that's been dealt to that family ... you'd say no family can endure that much," Self said.

Self said he'd abide by any decision Darnell made. His uncle and mom convinced him to remain in college.

Good decision.

"He is playing now without a lot of things weighing on his mind," Edred Jackson said. "Darnell is a kid you never know what is really on his mind. Ask him and you may never get the full understanding. I can definitely see he is having fun. He is not holding back. He sees the sky is the limit.

"I tell him, 'You work hard at something and good things will come out of it.'"

'Nobody can stop him'

So many good things are happening — Darnell, whose middle name is Edred, has had more highlight-reel plays this year than his previous three combined — his own teammates are in awe.

"He's doing whatever he wants to do," junior Brandon Rush said. "Scoring, rebounding, passing, dunking ... whatever he wants. He's gotten so much better. Nobody can stop him. He's always smiling, never depressed. I think there was a lot more on his mind last year."

"Darnell," fellow senior big man Sasha Kaun said simply, "is a beast."

A big, lovable beast.

"I like the way the fans have connected to him. I think they are drawn to him after all the stuff he's been through," Self said.

KU fans gave Darnell a prolonged standing ovation after his spin move and layup and ensuing free throw versus Yale.

"Everybody at KU has a sense of pride about his progress. They watched him go through everything from start to finish. It's a special story," Self added.

A story that may continue beyond this season.

Shawn Jackson says she's heard from some agents who may want to represent Darnell once his KU career is complete.

"They say, 'I enjoy watching him play.' They can talk to me. I say I'm not ready for all of that," Shawn said, noting Darnell is focused only on KU.

"We're on the same page. Right now we are worrying about every game," she said.

"Nah," Jackson said, asked if he was an NBA prospect. He's listed as a second-round choice on NBAdraft.net. "I don't know anything about showing up on the boards of the NBA. If it happens, it happens. I can't predict the future. I just stay focused and keep playing."

You know he will keep smiling.

"He's always had that smile. Even in bad times he could throw that smile out there," uncle Edred said. "It's been a shield a long time. Now he's letting his guard down. He's enjoying life." KU

"Out of the blue, it just changed for me. Coach (Bill) Self always tells me, 'Don't get too comfortable with yourself. We need to stay focused as a team, and when we're out here, just give everything you have.'"

JACKSON STAYS OUT OF TROUBLE

JANUARY 22, 2008 / BY TOM KEEGAN

FOR ALL THE THINGS TO MARVEL AT ON THIS UNDEFEATED KANSAS UNIVERSITY BASKETBALL TEAM, DARNELL JACKSON WORKING SO HARD AND STILL FINDING THE TIME TO SMILE SO OFTEN ON THE COURT RANKS NEAR THE TOP.

The explanation, in Jackson's mind, is quite simple. Compared to most of his friends with whom he hung out while growing up in Oklahoma City, he has plenty about which to smile. Twice this week, he'll have 16,300 voices cheering him. He has teammates with whom he shares a close bond. He has freedom.

Jackson said his "best friend" and high school teammate can't say the same.

"Right now, he's locked up," Jackson said before Monday's practice. "He's in jail. ... He was getting recruited by teams. He just wanted to be a gangster, I guess. ... I saw him over the summer at the mall. When I came back for Christmas break, he got locked up. All my friends I grew up with, they're all in jail, except one."

Jackson is such a kind, thoughtful sort it's difficult to picture so many he considered close friends going so wrong. How did it happen?

"I don't know," Jackson said. "I thought we were all going to make it one day. We all just hung out together, and when we were at school, some guys wanted to go the other way. My mom made sure she stayed on me. She didn't want me to go down that road."

That's one of many reasons every day is Mother's Day for Jackson. She kept him on the right path, one that has led to him having the time of his life as a starter for the undefeated, second-ranked Jayhawks.

Jackson said he has lost touch with friends now living behind bars.

"I don't even know where they're at," he said. "One of them is in California. A couple of them are down in Dallas."

Meanwhile, Jackson is making the most of the opportunities afforded a hard-working student-athlete. The decibels he generates from Allen Fieldhouse crowds show what a positive impression he's leaving on everyone associated with Kansas athletics. That can only help him in life.

His statistics, though impressive, merely hint at his value. Seeing someone so big play with so much enthusiasm has an energizing effect on the team. Jackson leads KU with 7.1 rebounds per game and ranks third with a scoring average of 12.3 points. His .672 shooting percentage is the most remarkable individual statistic on the team, considering many of his shots are 15-foot jumpers.

Jackson averages 24.2 minutes per game, compared to 15.3 last season.

"I thought my role was going to be the same," he said. "Out of the blue, it just changed for me. Coach (Bill) Self always tells me, 'Don't get too comfortable with yourself. We need to stay focused as a team, and when we're out here, just give everything you have.' That's what I try to do for him. I'm just thankful coach Self gives me the chance to play. I told him before the (Missouri) game, I just told him, 'Thank you. Thanks for everything you've done for me.'"

Jackson's advice for staying on the right road should be heeded by all young people tempted by the slippery slope that is the wrong side of the law: "When I see guys who don't want to do anything positive with their lives, I just try to make sure to avoid that." KU

RUSSELL ROBINSON

[AKA] **RUSS ROB**
[POSITION] **GUARD**
[YEAR] **SENIOR**
[NUMBER] **3**

HEIGHT	WEIGHT	PTS
6' 1"	205	291
FG %	3PT %	FT %
.424	.318	.779
PPG	ASSISTS	STEALS
7.3	162	79

Full Name: Russell Robinson, Jr.
Birthplace: Bronx, New York
Hometown: New York, New York
High School: Rice
Major: Communication Studies

If he was not the worst dunker on the team, he was close. His shot is not as pure as most of his teammates' and his numbers don't look like those of a starter for a national champion. So why is it that teammates considered Robinson as valuable as any member of the team? Because he made them all better, delivered the ball to them where they wanted it and when they needed it. He relieved pressure from them all by taking the toughest perimeter defensive assignment. He always made himself the fifth scoring option. In short, he was the perfect teammate. »

Nick Krug

"He is a pretty good player," Robinson said of Mayo, who missed 15 of 21 shots and bricked eight of 11 threes, thanks in large part to Robinson, also referred to as the heart and soul of KU's team.

ROBINSON PROVIDES STICKY 'D' ON MAYO

DECEMBER 3, 2007 / BY GARY BEDORE

LOS ANGELES — MORE THAN ONCE, RUSSELL ROBINSON HAS BEEN CALLED THE "GLUE" OF KANSAS UNIVERSITY'S BASKETBALL TEAM.

O.J. Mayo now knows why.

Robinson, the Jayhawks' 6-foot-1, 205-pound guard from New York, stuck to Mayo — who is four inches taller but weighs the same — throughout the Jayhawks' 59-55 victory at Galen Center.

"He is a pretty good player," Robinson said of Mayo, who missed 15 of 21 shots and bricked eight of 11 threes, thanks in large part to Robinson, also referred to as the heart and soul of KU's team.

"He can get his shot whenever, but I think the main thing today is he played all 40 minutes. He was tired at the end," Robinson added.

Mayo did hoist some closely guarded, ill-advised treys.

"He settled for a lot of shots, a lot of threes. That made my job easier," Robinson said.

Robinson — he had five points and two steals with four turnovers and an assist — shook his head when asked if he studied reams of tape on Mayo leading up to the game.

"No more than anybody else," Robinson said. "I've known him a long time, from my AAU days. I've seen him play a lot."

So where does Mayo rank of all the guys he has guarded?

"He's right up there. But today was not one of his better days," Robinson said.

Two of KU's big men had mixed feelings about Mayo.

"He's just unbelievable," said Sasha Kaun. "He can get any shot anytime he wants. Russell did a great job on him."

KU forward Darnell Jackson, who grabbed a career-best 13 rebounds, noted: "He's just a regular guy. I don't see anything impressive about him.

"He's a player. I respect him as a player. Other guys shouldn't give him that much respect on the court because if you love to compete, go out there and compete against him.

"He's just another player. He's just like us. He puts on a jersey, a practice jersey, just like everybody else every day."

Robinson guarded Mayo for 33 minutes. Rodrick Stewart and Mario Chalmers helped out during the times Robinson received a breather. KU

Thad Allender

UMKC
1
UMKC
KANSAS
att

KANSAS
3

UPCOMING EVENTS
KANSAS
3
TEXAS A&M
12

VICTORIES FOCUS FOR ROBINSON

NOVEMBER 1, 2007 / BY WILLIAM CROSS

EVERYONE ON THE KANSAS UNIVERSITY BASKETBALL TEAM, IT SEEMS, HAS A DIFFERENT OPINION OF RUSSELL ROBINSON'S BEST ATTRIBUTE.

But whatever his best skill is, Robinson's teammates are positive the senior point guard doesn't get enough credit for it.

"I think he shoots better than most people give him credit for," fellow senior guard Jeremy Case said.

"Russell is one of the strongest guys out here. I definitely don't think he gets enough credit for that," freshman Tyrel Reed lamented.

"I really think that Russell views his play on one thing, and that is wins and losses," coach Bill Self said. "A lot of people think they have to score, but I think Russell cares about winning."

Though Self sees it as a strength, Robinson's selflessness may be the very reason he is — to his fellow Jayhawks, anyway — so under appreciated.

Robinson, who started 35 of the Jayhawks' 38 games last season, is part of a six-man senior class that also includes key frontcourt contributors Sasha Kaun and Darnell Jackson. His goals this season reasonably could include defending his starting job or winning his third straight Big 12 tournament title, but Robinson says his focus is singular.

"I just want to leave Kansas with a ring," he said, "so they'll look back, and everybody will remember our senior class."

Last season, Robinson was a junior on a team with no seniors. Though experienced in the role of elder statesman, he said his niche this year would be different.

"There's something about seniors that's great for teams," he said. "Everyone has matured."

This season, the majority of backcourt minutes likely will be divided among Robinson, junior Mario Chalmers and sophomore Sherron Collins. Robinson, staying true to his role as a senior mentor, views the crowding as an opportunity rather than a competition. He sees Collins, more than other underclassmen, as his protege.

"Me and Russell, on the court, we understand each other," Collins said. "I'm never afraid to ask him for questions or ask him for help. I think he looks at me a different way because of the way I lead and the way I listen and try to take everything in. I look at him as a big brother."

Beloved by teammates and coaches, Robinson continues to earn their respect with his play. Though he averaged just 7.2 points per game last season, he led the team with 161 assists — no small feat on a team with Chalmers, Collins and passing aficionado Julian Wright on the same court. With Wright gone to the NBA and frontcourt scoring machine Darrell Arthur taking his place, Robinson could eclipse last year's assist total.

The part of Robinson's game that has impressed Reed, however, is his ability to drive to the hoop.

"He's really hard to guard when he has the ball," Reed said. "I just try to watch him and how he gets to the lane."

Drives the lane, racks up assists, earns teammates' respect, wins conference titles. What more could you want from a point guard?

Don't answer — Robinson already knows. For all of the success this year's senior class already has experienced, Robinson says he has had only "a taste."

"They want to go out as being recognized as one of the most winning classes," Self acknowledged. KU

Nick Krug

Recruited to Kansas by Roy Williams, he never got a chance to play for the coach who might or might not have found a spot for him as a role-player off the bench. Bill Self was a college teammate of Jeremy's father, Winn Case. Self recruited quicker, stronger guards than Case and the Oklahoma native never was able to crack the rotation. Teammates marveled over his outstanding long-range shooting in practice. It didn't often surface in games. Yet, on his last chance, his final game in Allen Fieldhouse, the personable shooter caught fire on a memorable Senior Night, driving the crowd wild. »

Thad Allender

HEIGHT	WEIGHT	PTS
6' 1"	190	47
FG %	3PT %	FT %
.378	.379	1.000
PPG	ASSISTS	STEALS
1.6	28	7

JEREMY CASE

[AKA] **CASE FACE**
[POSITION] **GUARD**
[YEAR] **SENIOR**
[NUMBER] **10**

Full Name: Jeremy Daryl Case
Birthplace: McAlester, Oklahoma
Hometown: McAlester, Oklahoma
High School: McAlester
Major: Bachelor's in Communication Studies (2007)

Nick Krug

"I hope people realize that just because people are sitting on the bench doesn't mean we can't play. It's just that the people who are playing are great. We have some really great players."

A CASE STUDY IN DEPTH

MARCH 4, 2008 / BY TOM KEEGAN

TO APPRECIATE FULLY HOW MUCH TALENT A BASKETBALL PLAYER MUST POSSESS TO EARN A SPOT IN THE ROTATION IN AN ELITE BASKETBALL PROGRAM SUCH AS KANSAS UNIVERSITY'S REQUIRES MORE THAN WATCHING DARRELL ARTHUR SKY TO SLAM HOME AN ALLEY-OOP. IT TAKES MORE THAN WITNESSING SHERRON COLLINS PUNCTUATE A BLURRY COAST-TO-COAST TRIP WITH A REVERSE LAY-IN KISSED OFF THE GLASS.

It takes Jeremy Case, who opened a window for 16,300 basketball nuts to see just how good a player needs to be to earn regular playing time at Kansas. Case never did get that time, but that doesn't mean he's not a terrific basketball player.

His strength and quickness didn't quite match that of the guards who played ahead of him at KU, yet his final night at the court that for four years he called home, usually from the bench, wasn't about how Case didn't measure up. It was about his uncanny shooting ability and improved play-making skills, his strong confidence and smart decision-making.

For Case, this night was about dominating a three-minute stretch in the second half of a 109-51 victory against a Texas Tech team that two days earlier had defeated Texas.

Afterward, Case talked about the chills hitting a trio of three-pointers gave him in a span of 2:24 midway through the second half. Thousands were chilling up with him. The kid everyone so badly wanted to see catch fire did. In a span of 3:02, Kansas outscored Tech, 16-4. Case had nine points and two assists that led to five points by the time the last grain of sand dropped in the egg timer.

Case made everybody in the place lose their minds.

The last time Case felt adrenaline flow as furiously as it did when he hit the third?

"I can't even remember," he said at first.

Then his memory finished scanning the years.

"Never, never felt that way," he said. "The crowd was so loud, I couldn't hear myself think. It was amazing."

In making the first start of his career, Case joined seniors Darnell Jackson, Sasha Kaun, Russell Robinson, and Rodrick Stewart. They played the first 3:37, settling the butterflies. They appeared together briefly late in the game, also, but it was between those stretches that they distinguished themselves.

Robinson, the perfect teammate, had the perfect night. He made all five field-goal attempts, all three three-point shots and both free throws. The five seniors combined for 50 points in 82 minutes. Remarkably, they generated 42 points on just 24 field-goal attempts. They made eight of 11 three-point shots.

Case deserves the most credit for a clutch performance, considering it was his first start and last chance to show he really is the phenomenal shooter that teammates who witness him daily in practice always have boasted that he is.

He doesn't play, but that doesn't mean he can't play. He can. Now there's no reason for anybody ever to doubt that.

"To play at one of the top schools is very hard," said Case, who graduated last spring. "You have to fight, fight, fight. I hope people realize that just because people are sitting on the bench doesn't mean we can't play. It's just that the people who are playing are great. We have some really great players."

On his final night in Allen Fieldhouse, Case was one of them. KU

CASE ACCUSTOMED TO 'OLD' JOKES

FIFTH-YEAR SENIOR REALLY ISN'T 36; HE JUST SEEMS THAT, UH, ADVANCED

NOVEMBER 1, 2007 / BY JESSE TEMPLE

JEREMY CASE HAS HEARD THE TEASING. HE KNOWS WHAT GIVES TEAMMATES REASON TO LAUGH AT HIS EXPENSE.

Jeremy Case is old.

"There's always little jokes," he said. "Like, 'Case is 36,' and stuff like that. 'I've been here 10 years.'"

Actually, Case isn't much older than most of his teammates. He turns 23 the second week of November. It just seems like he's 36 years old.

That's because this year will be Case's fifth go-round in the Kansas University men's basketball program. After his freshman season ended in 2004, he decided to red-shirt and retain a year of eligibility.

"It mainly was, we had a lot of guys coming back, and my chances of getting to play a lot were very slim," Case said. "I wanted to save that year, get stronger and get better."

As a result of that decision, Case already has put in his four years of school and earned an undergraduate degree. He graduated in May with a degree in communication studies.

"It was a great experience walking through the bell and walking down the hill seeing everybody," Case said of the graduation ceremony. "It was kind of like a weight off my shoulders. Just, I made it through, got my degree, and it felt good."

Now, Case is enrolled in classes again — this time in graduate school in sports management. He said the difference between graduate and undergraduate school is drastic.

"I feel like I have a lot more time," Case said. "I can get in extra shooting without being tired. I can get more sleep. It seems a lot more relaxing."

With Case the only current KU player to have earned his degree already, one might assume he's the most advanced Jayhawk in age. Lost in all the ribbing from teammates, though, is the fact that Case isn't even the oldest one on the team. That distinction goes to fellow senior Rodrick Stewart, who is actually more than five months older than Case. But Stewart, who transferred in to KU from Southern California, said he doesn't hear nearly the same wise-cracking as Case does.

"We have a real funny team, so we just love to have fun," Stewart said, "but we definitely do make fun of him."

Case doesn't appear too concerned about it, though. He knows it's all in good fun. He said while he hears plenty of comments, his teammates know they can count on him for just about anything.

"I've got respect from the guys," Case said. "They understand that I've been through a lot, so when they have questions, they ask."

Senior Sasha Kaun said Case certainly has earned the players' respect.

"He's been great," Kaun said. "He's a great guy and a really nice person."

With the admiration of teammates, a degree in hand and another one in the works, Case already is a success story, even if things don't pan out the way he wants on the court this year.

Not bad for a guy who's almost 23, going on 36. KU

Nick Krug

"I've got respect from the guys," Case said. "They understand that I've been through a lot, so when they have questions, they ask."

HEIGHT	WEIGHT	PTS
5' 11"	205	315
FG %	3PT %	FT %
.462	.362	.776
PPG	ASSISTS	STEALS
9.3	105	39

SHERRON COLLINS

[AKA] S DOT/RON RON
[POSITION] GUARD
[YEAR] SOPHOMORE
[NUMBER] 4

Full Name: Sherron Marlon Collins
Birthplace: Chicago, Illinois
Hometown: Chicago, Illinois
High School: Crane
Major: Undecided

Broken foot. Bruised kneecap. Tonsillitis. For the second season in a row, the in-your-face point guard from Chicago had trouble staying healthy. He got it together just in time, and when he was healthy Kansas played at a different speed. He leads with his chin and never retreats. To the rest of the nation, Memphis point guard Derrick Rose was the flavor of the month, the potential No. 1 overall pick who couldn't be stopped. To Collins, he was just another foe from the rough-and-tumble Chicago Public League. »

Thad Allender

JAYHAWKS BETTER WITH HEALTHY COLLINS

MARCH 9, 2008 / BY TOM KEEGAN

COLLEGE STATION, TEXAS — IT HAS BEEN AWHILE SINCE THE "WHAT'S WRONG WITH KANSAS?" QUESTION THAT LED TO SO MUCH INSOMNIA HAS BEEN ASKED WITH ANY CREDIBILITY. IT ALSO HAS BEEN AWHILE SINCE SHERRON COLLINS' KNEE HAS PREVENTED HIM FROM PERFORMING HIGH-SPEED MAGIC SHOWS WITH THE BASKETBALL.

A coincidence? Uh, no.

Collins steered the Jayhawks to a 72-55 regular-season-finale victory Saturday against a Texas A&M team that just didn't have the speed to keep pace.

With Collins looking more like his healthy self, Kansas defeated Kansas State, Texas Tech and Texas A&M by an average margin of victory of 29.3 points, a figure inflated by the 58-point slaughter of Tech. During that season-ending stretch, Collins averaged 14.7 points, had 14 assists and two turnovers.

He never was better than Saturday, when in 32 minutes he totaled 13 points with seven assists and not a single turnover.

Collins sends a defense scrambling in a way no other KU player can, and he, more than anybody on the offensive side, was responsible for the greatest statistical disparity on the box score, a 44-12 points-in-the-paint advantage for the Jayhawks.

Former Kansas point guard Mark Turgeon, who coached against his alma mater for the first time Saturday, marveled at the influence Collins had on the game.

"That's a quick team," Turgeon said. "Texas is fast and quick, but that's another level today. And when Sherron Collins plays like that, boy, it could be their year, if he stays healthy. He was really, really good today."

Foot surgery sidelined Collins early in the season, and a bruised knee slowed him more recently. Without him at his best, Kansas looked as if it lacked energy. What it really lacked was the advantage of having a man who consistently blows by his man and basically sets up a 5-on-4 advantage.

When Collins blew by his man, he knew where to get the ball, feeding Darrell Arthur (16 points). Mario Chalmers (16 points, four steals), per usual doing a little bit of everything at both ends, also had a big day.

"I thought Shady was great in the first half," KU coach Bill Self said of Arthur. "Mario was great the majority of the game. But there was a stretch in the second half it was Sherron's game. He controlled the game. That's something people that follow us know we haven't had consistently at all this year, and, hopefully, we can continue to get better and progress and get him playing with that full head of steam that he has. I don't know if he's got an extra gear, but he's so low to the ground."

And so clever with the ball at such high speeds. Once, Collins drove into a crowded lane, and the only way he could get where he needed to go was to dribble behind his back, and he did it so quickly those who blinked probably missed it.

With a healthy Collins, KU's two greatest strengths, quickness and depth, become so much louder.

"They've got seven or eight starters, it seems like," Turgeon said. "There's no drop-off when they sub. You line us up in a foot race, it's not even close. They're fast."

And seemingly peaking just in time. KU

Nick Krug

BLACKMAN
25
1977-1981
OHLDE
3
2000-2004
WECKER
53
2001-2005
KANSAS
24
30

4
24

4

KANSAS
4

KANSAS
4

"I told him, 'Be the beast that you are,'" Harris said. "And he did. He did fantastic today. I think he's back."

JAYHAWKS' COLLINS PLAYS LIKE A 'BEAST'

MARCH 2, 2008 / BY RYAN GREENE

THE PAIN THAT LINGERS LESS AND LESS EACH PASSING DAY IN HIS RIGHT KNEE WAS THE FARTHEST THING FROM SHERRON COLLINS' MIND SATURDAY NIGHT.

Sure, the adrenaline of the situation once the game got under way had something to do with that. It was flowing for about two straight hours as Kansas University trounced Kansas State, 88-74, in Allen Fieldhouse.

But, as Collins admits, the presence of family made the ultimate difference.

"My mom came down, my son's down, so everything was happy for me," said the sophomore guard, whose filled-up stat line was highlighted by 18 points on 7-of-12 shooting. "Just this game took my mind off my knee. I wanted to beat K-State, but it was a plus to have my mom here."

Stacy Harris and 10-month-old Sherr'mari Marlon Collins arrived in Lawrence on Saturday, and the three of them spent the afternoon in Sherron's apartment.

The presence of Sherr'mari was enough to put a smile on Collins' face, but mom still had some words of wisdom.

"I told him, 'Be the beast that you are,'" Harris said. "And he did. He did fantastic today. I think he's back."

Few would have a hard time arguing the spark plug off the bench looks more and more now like the guy who totaled 32 points and 10 assists in the season's first two games before going down because of a stress fracture in his foot.

Collins' health has improved consistently since he went scoreless in 11 minutes Saturday at Oklahoma State, but against Kansas State he looked like the Collins of old for the first time in a while as the bone bruise in his right knee continues to fade.

The 18 points he totaled included a 3-of-7 showing from deep. He also had four assists (to just one turnover), four steals and three rebounds to his credit in 29 minutes. The amount of playing time tied a season-high that Collins set against UMKC on Nov. 11 and at Kansas State on Jan. 30.

"I wouldn't say (it felt like) years (since I've felt like that)," Collins said with a smile. "But I'd say it feels like months.

"Wednesday (at Iowa State), I didn't feel like I was tonight, but it was just turning around quick. I could feel it Wednesday. It was getting better. I was able to do stuff I wasn't able to do earlier in the week. Two days (later), it turned around."

And at a time in the season when Final Four hopefuls aim to be playing their best brand of basketball, Collins at full strength is a welcome sign for coach Bill Self.

"The last two days, he's moved better. The doctor says he's just going to keep getting better, the bruise is going to continue to heal, and he'll be where he's pain-free here real soon," Self said. "But I thought he was great tonight. That's what we've been missing for the most part of the entire year, to have somebody that's that explosive who can change a game, and he certainly was a great spark tonight." KU

clockwise from top left: Thad Allender, Nick Krug, Nick Krug, Thad Allender

When teammates run into problems with their computers, they turned to Sasha. When the team was having trouble containing a post player, the coach turned to the 6-foot-11 senior who had been a starter from his sophomore year on until being replaced by Darnell Jackson early in the national-title season. Coming off the bench brought out the best in the friendly center from Tomsk, Russia, who left home at the age of 16 for Florida to become a better basketball player. The courageous move paid off for Kaun, whose huge game against Davidson won't soon be forgotten. »

Thad Allender

HEIGHT	WEIGHT	PTS
6' 11"	250	284
FG %	3PT %	FT %
.619	.000	.541
PPG	ASSISTS	STEALS
7.1	12	17

SASHA KAUN

[AKA] **SASHA**
[POSITION] **CENTER**
[YEAR] **SENIOR**
[NUMBER] **24**

Full Name: Alexander Kaun
Birthplace: Tomsk, Russia
Hometown: Melbourne, Florida
High School: Florida Air Academy
Major: Computer Science

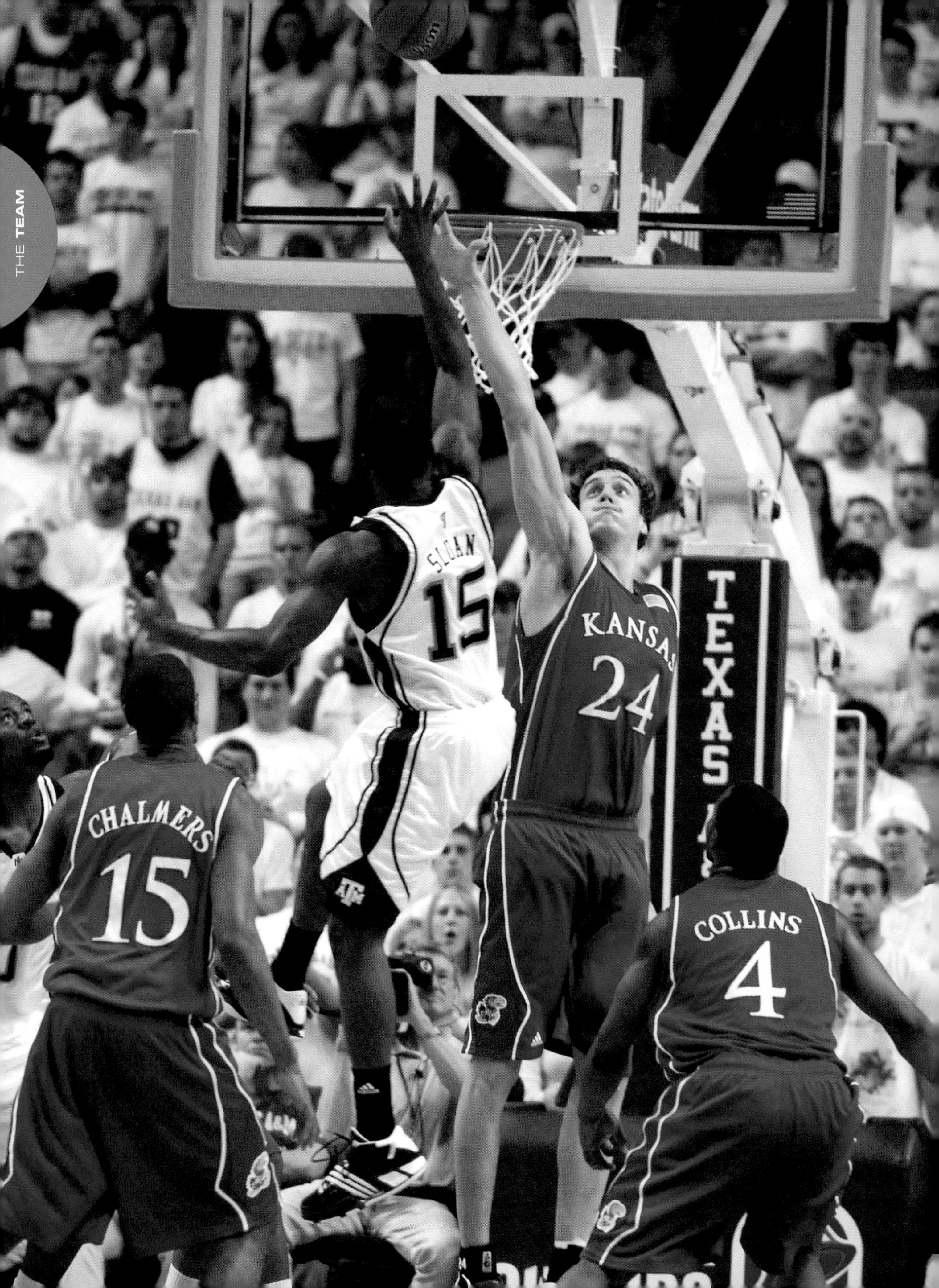
SLOAN
15
KANSAS
24
TEXAS
CHALMERS
15
COLLINS
4

KAUN INSPIRES HUNTED

MARCH 31, 2008 / BY TOM KEEGAN

DETROIT — THE ROAD TO THE FINAL FOUR TOOK A DETOUR TO TOMSK, RUSSIA, WHERE A BOY LEFT HOME AT THE AGE OF 16 TO PURSUE A BASKETBALL DREAM.

Sasha Kaun, undeterred by the weight of expectations, the pressures of being the hunted, the enormity of it all, played the game of his life Sunday evening inside Ford Field, where 57,563 were treated to a David vs. Goliath game that went down to the final sling-shot, wide left.

By the time an extremely well-guarded three-pointer from Davidson's Jason Richards hit the backboard, Kaun was watching, his penchant for missing free throws making him too big a risk to be on the floor. Yet, without 20 minutes of sheer aggression from the 6-foot-11 reserve center, Kansas would not be going to the Final Four to take on the school's former coach, Roy Williams, and the North Carolina Tar Heels.

"Probably the longest shot I've seen in my life, just being in the air for so long," Kaun said, his Russian eyes smiling so brightly. "Just relieved when I saw it hit the backboard. Just happy after that."

A glance at a scoreboard that showed Kansas 59, Davidson 57, was needed just to make sure it was over. That's how hard it was to kill a giant-killer that brought a 25-game winning streak into the game.

"I just wanted to make sure that I hurried up and shook hands, and the officials left the court so they couldn't put any more time back on the clock," KU coach Bill Self said.

Relief spread throughout the Kansas bench and in the stands. Self was on both knees, praying his only means of control in the final seconds, and dropped forward when the shot missed.

For much of the game, it was easy to tell the hunters, tiny Davidson College, from the hunted, No. 1 Kansas, even in the stands, where the backers of Wildcats wore red, supporters of Kansas blue. The red spectators stood throughout, bringing such festive energy to the event. The band played the team's theme song — Neil Diamond's "Sweet Caroline" — and the fans sang along. They were having a blast, so happy to be there in new late-March territory, so loose. The blue section appeared more tense, begging for a shot that would give them relief, free them from the tension of it all, and when the shots they so badly wanted rolled off the rim, they groaned, flashbacks of past near misses haunting them.

The hunters played with nothing to lose, trapping the ball in the post with such vigor, never hesitating to take a shot. The hunted played with a tightness that early in the game resulted in players missing shots they normally make and then late in the game passing up shots they normally take.

"This game has a different feel to it than a lot of other games," said KU coach Bill Self, who improved to 1-4 in Elite Eight games. "I thought we were loose. I thought everything was great. But I even talked to our guys in there afterward. It just has a different feel because everybody knows the stakes are so high. Playing Davidson, you know, even though it's not the same 'Wow!' factor with the name of their school, not being from a BCS conference or whatever, I think in some ways maybe puts a little subtle pressure on you. Our guys didn't handle it great, but we were tough enough to get the win, which is all that matters."

And through it all, there was Kaun, the least offensively gifted of the nine players who appeared in the game for Kansas, clapping his hands to demand the ball, tossing bodies aside to get into position for rebounds, challenging so many shots and blocking one, not looking anything but energized by the heat of the moment.

Kansas played a terrific defensive game, most notably on the final possession, and made superstar Stephen Curry work so hard for his 25 shots. Still, KU needed all of Kaun's field goals to fall for that effort not to go down as a footnote swallowed by tales of failure. Kaun contributed 13 points and six rebounds and shot 6-of-6 from the field, 1-of-3 from the line.

His offensive output came in handy because Davidson reserve Bryant Barr evoked bad memories of Texas Tech's Darryl Dora and Marchello Vealy of Oral Roberts, lesser-known players for whom the basket grew so large in victories against Kansas.

In the second half, Barr scored 11 points and made all four of his shots, three from beyond the arc. He entered averaging 5.1 points. That's the stuff of which upsets are made. It didn't happen, which left Davidson's players and coaches wearing the boxing gloves, punching their mirrors, the way it always happens when such a big victory falls just short. Tough business. »

Nick Krug

(CONTINUED)

Sasha Kaun, undeterred by the weight of expectations, the pressures of being the hunted, the enormity of it all, played the game of his life...

"Every player and I will beat ourselves up about what we did or didn't do because every play counts," Davidson coach Bob McKillop said. "We believe that. That's the way we coach. That's the way we play. I made the mistake (on the final play) of not realizing to tell our guys to set the ball screen with the big rather than with Chalmers guarding. That did not come out in the huddle. That's the mistake I made. Yet, if Jason Richards makes that shot, we're geniuses and we're in the Final Four."

Instead, Self and the Jayhawks are in the Final Four, and the easy-angle hunters must find a new man to brand "best coach never to make it to the Final Four," a left-handed compliment Self was happy to shed. His team no longer has to play with the burden of being the hunted. For the first time, all four No. 1 seeds advanced to the Final Four. North Carolina is ranked the highest No. 1 seed, Kansas the lowest.

The last time Kansas entered a game with this strong an underdog label, not that it's a huge one, came Nov. 25, 2006, in Las Vegas, against defending national champion Florida. Julian Wright and Darrell Arthur took it to the Gators, 82-80.

"I think we should have a great week of practice and preparation," Self said. "The hard part is just beginning, but in our guys' minds there's been a weight that has been lifted, which should free us up a little bit."

They survived as the hunted and are eager to thrive as the hunters. KU

from top: Nick Krug, Thad Allender

KAUN FINDS TOUCH AT FREE THROW LINE

JANUARY 4, 2008 / BY GARY BEDORE

SIX GAMES INTO THE SEASON, BILL SELF HAD SEEN ENOUGH.

It was time for a coach/player chat with Kansas University senior center Sasha Kaun, who bricked three of four free throws in a Nov. 28 rout of Florida Atlantic.

The three misses dropped the 6-foot-11 Kaun to 10-of-27 from the line for a Shaq-like 37 percent.

"We told him he was 0-for-0," KU coach Self said. "(Since then) he's shot it pretty well."

Kaun hit three of four free throws in the ensuing game against Southern California and in the past seven games has made 15 of 22 for 68.2 percent.

"Right before the USC game, coach said, 'Your free throws start now. Step up and make the free throws,''' Kaun said.

Before missing two without a make last Saturday against Yale, the career 49.8 percent shooter had made 15 of his last 20 for 75 percent in six games.

"I think it's really mental for me," Kaun said. "In practice I shoot them really well, 75 to 80 percent. I try to relax and do what I do in practice."

Self, whose team has made 166 of 266 for 62.8 percent, believes confidence is key to making the unguarded shot.

"He's been working on it. He seems more relaxed at the line," Self said of Kaun. "I think he had lost some confidence when he didn't shoot his free throws well. It kind of affected his total game. He's more a presence now than earlier in the season."

Kaun, a former starter who has given way to Darnell Jackson and come off the bench the last eight games, said it's just a coincidence he's played well in a relief role.

"We still get the same minutes," Kaun said. "We play three or four bigs. Not starting may relieve a little more pressure, but it doesn't matter whether you start or not. It's been good for our team I think."

Self said starting versus coming off the bench "is totally irrelevant. I don't think it's any big deal. He has been more productive of late. I don't think coming off the bench has anything to do with it.

"Throughout his career, he's gone through phases where he's been very productive and phases he's had a little bit of a dry spell. Now he's certainly on an up-tick."

Self likes the fact he doesn't have to worry about ego issues on this team. Sherron Collins, who also comes off the bench, likely would be starting for any other team in the league.

Nick Krug

"These guys don't care who starts," Self said. "Probably the best thing about our team is guys like each other so much."

Don't expect any lineup changes soon ... as long as the team stays healthy.

"This is who we are. I don't see an immediate change. Injuries or situations can change that. I like the way we're playing in our rotation now," Self said.

That's fine with Kaun.

"It's my senior year. I'm focusing on having fun," he said. KU

RODRICK STEWART

[AKA] **R DOT**
[POSITION] **GUARD**
[YEAR] **SENIOR**
[NUMBER] **5**

HEIGHT	WEIGHT	PTS
6' 4"	200	92
FG %	3PT %	FT %
.493	.313	.607
PPG	ASSISTS	STEALS
2.8	47	13

Full Name: Rodrick Stewart
Birthplace: Aberdeen, Mississippi
Hometown: Seattle, Washington
High School: Rainier Beach
Major: African and African-American Studies

At the end of a public practice in the Alamodome the day before the national semifinal, he went up for a dunk, slipped on the floor and fractured his kneecap. Things didn't work out for Stewart as well as he had hoped when he transferred from USC after his freshman year. None of that mattered, though, when at the end of the national semi-final rout of North Carolina, KU fans began chanting "Rod-rick Ste-wart (clap, clap, clap, clap, clap), Rod-rick Stew-art (clap, clap, clap, clap, clap)." Sitting at the end of the bench, his crutches nearby, Stewart buried his face in his hands to catch the tears. »

Thad Allender

STEWART HAPPY TO HELP ANY WAY

JANUARY 26, 2008 / BY GARY BEDORE

KANSAS UNIVERSITY SENIOR GUARD RODRICK STEWART, WHO AVERAGED 17.1 MINUTES PER GAME DURING THE NONCONFERENCE SEASON, IS DOWN TO 8.0 MINUTES IN FOUR LEAGUE CONTESTS.

But, hey, who's counting?

Not team player Stewart, that is for sure.

"This is bigger than me. It's not about me," Stewart said simply.

The 6-foot-4, 200-pound defensive whiz from Seattle — he started seven games early-on as Brandon Rush was brought back slowly from offseason knee surgery — says he remains upbeat as ever entering today's 12:45 p.m. home battle against Nebraska.

"I still have the same attitude, the same mind-set as I had at the beginning of the season," said Stewart, who played 29 and 27 minutes in victories over Southern Cal and Arizona.

"It's not about what I am doing. It's all about winning."

Stewart, who also was counted on heavily during the six games Sherron Collins missed because of a foot injury, has averaged 4.2 points and 2.8 rebounds — while dishing 38 assists to 20 turnovers — in 19 games.

In league play, Stewart has scored four points and grabbed 10 rebounds total, while focusing on defense.

"Rodrick is an energy guy. He guards, guards, guards," sophomore Collins said. "He can guard the 4 (power forward) through the 1 (point guard). I think he takes pride in guarding. He does it really well."

"He's a great defensive player," junior guard Mario Chalmers noted. "He's playing a big role. He's not playing as many minutes as he was, (but) he's still effective when he gets in there.

"He gets rebounds that get us extra possessions. That's what we need. He gives us extra energy."

Stewart had four rebounds in nine minutes in last Saturday's 76-70 victory at Missouri and two in nine minutes of KU's 79-58 victory over Nebraska on Jan. 12 in Lincoln.

He spent some time shadowing Ryan Anderson, a 6-foot-4 sophomore out of Stewart's alma mater, Seattle's Rainier Beach High. Anderson scored 12 points off 4-of-12 shooting, 3-of-10 from three-point land.

"When you play a team like Nebraska, it will be a fast-paced game. They have a lot of guards, too," Stewart said.

He indicated his role is "to be aggressive when I'm out there. It comes down to guarding your man. It's really what we do. We can't worry about stuff they (Huskers, 11-5 overall, 0-3 league) run. If we guard like we can, we can take teams out of the offensive sets they run."

In the first meeting, 6-11 center Aleks Maric led the Huskers with 19 points off 7-of-12 shooting. Anderson was the only other Husker in double figures on a day NU hit 40 percent of its shots to KU's 53.8 mark.

"He is one of those guys that will be in the whole game unless he's in foul trouble," Stewart said of Maric, who averages a team-leading 16.6 points and 8.2 rebounds. "We've got to attack him, get him running, get him a little tired.

"It's going to be a good game. It's always hard to play somebody a second time. You can blow a team out the first game, the second game can be a totally different thing," Stewart added. "They have enough talent. They can adjust to a lot of the things we do. We will come out and do what we do, play defense, try to play through our bigs (on offense)."

KU coach Bill Self, who has been primarily using a seven-man rotation of late, said he has complete trust in Stewart.

"Rod gives us energy, toughness, steals extra possessions for us," Self said. "His role could be eight minutes a game to 20 minutes a game depending on personnel or foul issues. His role hasn't changed."

One of Stewart's roles is senior leader.

"Rod is a team player. Everybody loves him. He keeps us going," senior guard Russell Robinson said. "He's one of the locker room guys, keeping everybody together. He might not be getting the minutes on the court right now, but he will come in there, and when he does he changes the game for us."

Stewart's positive attitude rubs off on the rest of the players, junior Brandon Rush said.

"He's full of energy. He goes hard all the time in games and practice," Rush said. "He's always smiling. He's living a dream right now. He's at Kansas playing for the No. 2 team in the country. He's having a dream season."

Indeed ...

"It's definitely been fun," Stewart said of his final college season. "This isn't about me going in there trying to score or anything. It's about accepting your role. That's when you have great teams, when everybody can accept their role.

"I am not a selfish guy at all. We've got a deep team, a lot of guys who contribute every day in practice and in games.

"We're good. We've still got a long ways to go. We're getting there, though," Stewart concluded. KU

clockwise from top left: Nick Krug, Nick Krug, Thad Allender, Nick Krug

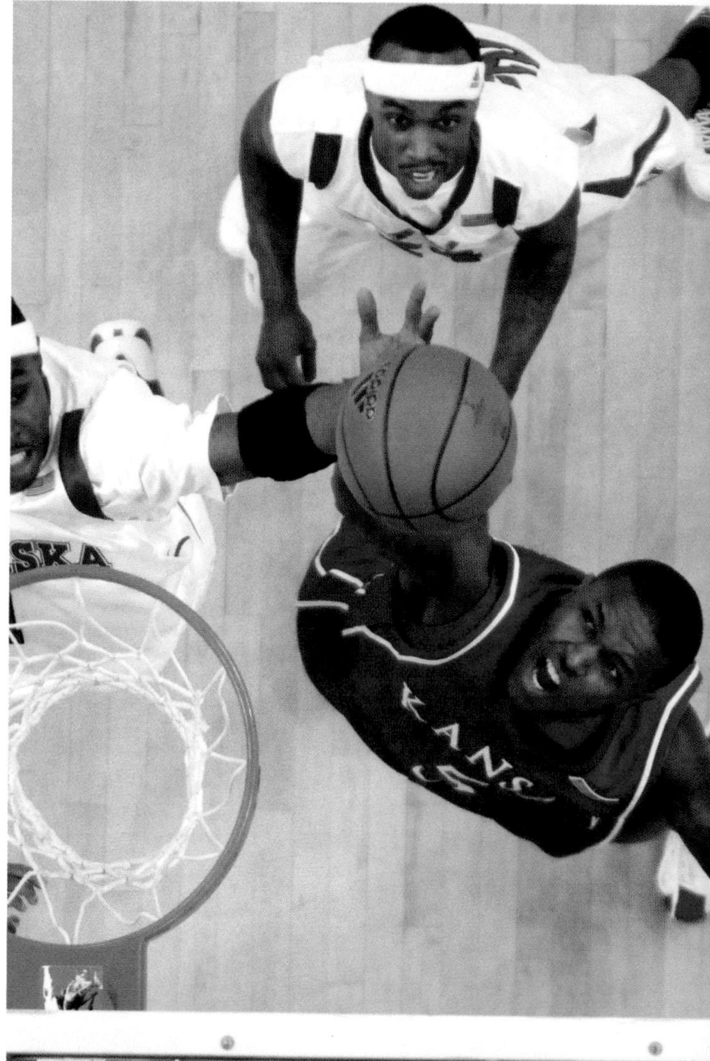

It's rare for an elite basketball program to have five seniors. It's far more common for the powerhouses to have players who arrive on campus with the sole purpose of trying to hone their games to the degree they can play for pay as soon as possible. As soon as they arrive, their goal is to leave. Such never was the case for the special senior class that proved to be the glue of the champions.

Darnell Jackson improved every year, never hearing the initials NBA attached to his name until he was a senior. Russell Robinson started for three seasons, ever the complementary player. Sasha Kaun played the best basketball of his career as a senior reserve after being a starter his sophomore and junior seasons. Jeremy Case stole the show on Senior Night, and Rodrick Stewart, in crutches at the Final Four, played well early in the year as Brandon Rush worked his way back from knee surgery.

The class will be remembered as the humble and hard-working backbone of a national championship. »

Nick Krug

SENIOR CLASS

NATIONAL CHAMPIONS
1922
THANK YOU
3,5,10,24,32,40
SENIORS

KANSAS

SENIORS EMBODY CLASS

MARCH 3, 2008 / BY TOM KEEGAN

WILL HE BE BACK NEXT SEASON? WILL HE HIRE AN AGENT, OR DO YOU THINK HE'LL HOLD OFF ON THAT, TEST THE WATERS AT THE DRAFT CAMP, AND THEN DECIDE WHETHER HE'LL ENTER HIS NAME INTO THE NBA DRAFT?

Such questions, rain clouds hovering over elite basketball programs across the map, can sap the old-fashioned, college enthusiasm out of the sport that warms our winters. Therein lies the beauty of the senior class that will be honored in tonight's Allen Fieldhouse finale. Thrill-killing questions never have been posed about Jeremy Case, Darnell Jackson, Sasha Kaun, Russell Robinson and Rodrick Stewart.

Case, recruited to Kansas by Roy Williams, redshirted a year and graduated last spring. The rest are on track to graduate this coming spring.

To a man, the five scholarship student-athletes, who will give senior speeches after tonight's game against Texas Tech, never did anything to leave the impression they viewed wearing a Kansas uniform as a means to achieve a more lucrative basketball end.

Bolting early in pursuit of NBA dollars never presented itself as a realistic option for them, which makes Jackson's development into a prospect projected by many to go in the second round of the draft all the more gratifying.

A reserve until early this season, Jackson has a terrific touch on his 15-foot jumper, yet only uses it to win, not to audition for NBA scouts. In the first five minutes of his second-to-last game in Allen Fieldhouse, an 88-74 victory against Kansas State, Jackson scored eight points and didn't take a shot from outside of two feet. He opened the half with a put-back slam and also scored on a short bank put-back, on an alley-oop dunk and on another dunk after he sealed his man, caught the pass, and executed a subtle move to avoid the help defender. No KU player has been more productive this season.

During last month's reunion celebration of 110 years of Kansas basketball, former KU star Ron Franz made a point to introduce himself to Jackson.

"You play every possession like it's your last," Franz told Jackson. "You play every game like it's your last."

Jackson will experience an important last tonight when he makes his final run through the tunnel.

When Robinson, Case, Stewart, Jackson and Kaun start, it won't be the force job it is on most Senior Night games. The five played together for a stretch early in November. Look for them to get off to a strong start, fueled by a grateful crowd that appreciates the effort this class of seniors put forth.

Robinson, missing New York, hung tough and grew up in a hurry after a frustrating freshman season. Every team needs a glue guy. Robinson makes the all-Elmer's team. Case never did earn a spot in the rotation and never did complain about that. Stewart, a transfer after a year at USC, rode the pine his first two seasons at Kansas, never stopped trying to get better and finally earned a spot in the rotation. Jackson's year-by-year growth, in the face of so much personal tragedy, embodies all that is good about college basketball. Kaun went from starter to reserve this season, a demotion, at least in name, that didn't poison his passion.

After tonight, they'll be gone from the Fieldhouse. Gone and not soon forgotten. KU

clockwise from top left: Thad Allender, Nick Krug, Thad Allender

THE FRESHMEN

Future star Cole Aldrich and role player candidate Tyrel Reed were the members of the freshmen class on scholarship, but that would have been difficult to guess based on the reaction of the crowds inside Allen Fieldhouse. It was Conner Teahan, long-range shooter extraordinaire, who generated the loudest crowd reactions. Fans began chanting his name as blowouts reached the final minutes. Their car rides home could wait. They had to see how many rainbow three-pointers Teahan would bury on this night. Would it be one, two or three? Each one would be greeted by a high-pitched mania, the co-eds roaring their approval the loudest for the shooting touch and hair style they so adored. »

Nick Krug

COLE ALDRICH

[AKA] **BIG C/SLAW/BIG COLE**
[POSITION] **CENTER**
[YEAR] **FRESHMAN**
[NUMBER] **45**

Full Name: Cole David Aldrich
Birthplace: Burnsville, Minnesota
Hometown: Bloomington, Minnesota
High School: Jefferson
Major: Undecided

The only reasonable assumption to draw from watching the freshman center struggle to keep up during the Late Night scrimmage could be summed up in three words: "Not this year." Flash forward nearly six months to the Alamodome. There was Aldrich abusing national Player of the Year Tyler Hansbrough of North Carolina, hitting baseline jumpers, blocking shots, muscling away rebounds. Clearly, a year of trading elbows daily in practice with three more seasoned players had accelerated Aldrich's development. All-Big 12 honors are in his not-too-distant future. »

HEIGHT	WEIGHT	PTS
6' 11"	240	112
FG %	3PT %	FT %
.518	.000	.684
PPG	ASSISTS	STEALS
2.8	5	11

Thad Allender

ALDRICH PROVES TOUGH

KU HOOPS FRESHMAN SHRUGS OFF PAIN

DECEMBER 16, 2007 / BY TOM KEEGAN

COLE ALDRICH LOOKED LIKE HE WAS EXECUTING MOVES HE LEARNED IN PRESEASON BOXING-WORKOUTS, BOBBING UP AND DOWN AS HE SHUFFLED OFF THE ALLEN FIELDHOUSE COURT.

Actually, he was weaving over to the corner cut man — make that the team trainer — after suffering a right hand injury at a recent Kansas University basketball practice.

"We were going fullcourt, and all of a sudden Cole starts hopping around. He said, 'Oww, my hand,' in his Minnesota accent," KU junior center Matt Kleinmann said with a smile.

"We thought it was a hangnail or something. We were like, 'C'mon, Cole, keep playing.' A couple minutes later we see it gushing (blood). It was like a movie injury."

The 6-foot-11, 240-pound Aldrich, who long ago earned his stripes for toughness by weathering coach Bill Self's basketball Boot Camp and holding his own in 1-on-1 sessions in the paint against veterans Sasha Kaun and Darnell Jackson, sliced his mitt battling Kaun for a rebound.

"When I came down, all I felt was pain in my hand. I looked down and all you could see was the whole webbing of my hand was ripped open. There's a big ol' rip. You don't see that every day," Aldrich said.

"I ran over to the sideline (yelling), 'Look at my hand, it's ripped open.' I put a few other choice words in there. It wasn't bleeding at first. Then it starts gushing blood. My whole hand was filled with blood. There was blood all over the place."

Aldrich — he tore open the skin on the front of his hand between his thumb and index finger — needed six stitches to close the wound.

Legend has it he wanted to continue practicing, but by the time he was patched, practice was over. He was on the court the next day, ready to go, wearing a heavy wrap which he has continued to wear the past several games.

Just another day at the office for Aldrich, deemed a "tough kid" by demanding coach Self.

"I don't want to rank him as the toughest (freshman) I've been around," Self said. "I do think this ... from where he was to where he is now, there's not been too many freshmen I've coached make that immediate amount of improvement in all areas, including his body. He's worked hard to get rid of all the body fat and redefine his body since he got here."

Self said that since Aldrich's arrival at KU last May, the player went from 270 pounds to his current weight of 240, thanks to a strict regimen of 6 a.m. daily workouts.

Three of the week's five 6 a.m. workouts included shadow boxing and cardio boxing training under the direction of Haskell's boxing coach.

"I went through a phase my junior year (at Jefferson High Bloomington, Minn). I got a stress fracture in my fibula on my left leg. I sat out a few weeks and started to put on a little weight," Aldrich said. "When I got here in the summer, the coaches said, 'We think it'd be a great thing to start losing a little weight, get a little more athletic and you'll be playing better.

"I did the boxing to get endurance, work on my

"When I came down, all I felt was pain in my hand. I looked down and all you could see was the whole webbing of my hand was ripped open. There's a big ol' rip. You don't see that every day," Aldrich said.

hands and footwork and lose some baby fat. I also met with our nutritionist and said, 'I'm trying to get down to a good playing weight. What foods can I eat to help me perform better?' I got a list of different foods to eat throughout the day, and we made a meal plan of what I could eat."

Though Aldrich has learned to love his fruits and vegetables in toning his body to the point Self says, "He looks good," the big guy admittedly slips once in a while.

"I do like my Doritos and whatnot," said Aldrich, who as part of his Minnesota vocabulary spices what seems like every other sentence with the word whatnot.

"I like everything. I love pickles, though. I've got a big jar of pickles in the room. I love 'em. I don't know why I love pickles, but I do."

On the court, Aldrich has been a factor as KU's fourth big man in his rookie season. He has averaged 3.0 points and 3.4 rebounds while logging an average of 8.8 minutes in KU's 31 games.

He has emerged lately in logging 10.7 minutes per game the last six games. Aldrich had 11 points with 11 rebounds on March 3 against Texas Tech and followed that with three points and two boards in 14 minutes in the regular-season finale versus Texas A&M. He had six points and four boards against Colorado on Feb. 16 and six points and nine boards versus Missouri on Feb. 4.

"I think he has a chance to have as productive a college career as those guys on the list, (also realizing) some of them may not be in school long," Self said of the league's all-freshman team of Michael Beasley, Bill Walker, Blake Griffin, James Anderson and DeAndre Jordan.

"By the time he gets out of here, he will be on those other teams," Self added of All-Big 12 first and second teams.

While Aldrich will be called upon on during this weekend's Big 12 tournament — KU opens against either Missouri or Nebraska at 6 p.m. Friday at Sprint Center — and the NCAAs, it will be next season when his minutes skyrocket.

KU will lose Kaun and Jackson to graduation, while Darrell Arthur is all but certain to declare for the NBA Draft.

That leaves Aldrich and walk-on Kleinmann, as well as newcomers Markieff Morris, Quintrell Thomas and possibly one more big man signee to roam the inside.

"Just a little, not much," Aldrich said, asked if he feels pressure to lead the big man group next season. "We trust coach with who we recruited. We've got a great amount of guys coming in, seems like 15 guys coming in. They are all great guys and even better players."

With KU's penchant to look inside then out, it's possible Aldrich could put up some dominating numbers his sophomore campaign.

"I guess I'd ask you what 'dominating' really is," Aldrich said. "Is dominating getting 10 rebounds a game? That would be a great goal, maybe one I could set for myself. That's something I can put on effort, going after every rebound that comes my way."

Aldrich said he plans to spend almost the entire summer in Lawrence.

"It's pretty much a great place to be," said Aldrich, who from May to August likely will be found at the Jaybowl when he's not playing hoops.

One of the world's tallest bowlers won a lifetime-activities-class competition in high school with a score of 204. His high score is 214.

"Straight power. I just throw a straight line drive down the middle," Aldrich said. "Some people think bowling is not that exciting. I love it. I grew up bowling. My grandpa was a really good bowler. He had a few 300 games. I was in a league from kindergarten to sixth grade.

"It's a way to get out and have fun. Some like to go out. Some like to play golf. I stink (at golf). I'm very tempted to get my own ball and own shoes. It could be a new thing, seeing me at the Jaybowl or whatnot."

He may like bowling and pickles and speak in a strange dialect (to these parts), but don't get the idea Aldrich is any kind of a flake. He's a respected member of this team.

"He's a smart player. People don't realize he's had to go through a lot of adversity," Kleinmann said. "As a heralded freshman coming out here, playing against some upperclassmen, he persevered, and he's playing quality minutes, too. He's going to be a great player at KU." KU

KU'S ALDRICH ON RISE

DECEMBER 16, 2007 / BY GARY BEDORE

KANSAS CITY, MO. — HE WAS BEHIND THE PLAY, AND THEN HE WAS THE PLAY. KANSAS UNIVERSITY RESERVE FRESHMAN CENTER COLE ALDRICH SLAMMED HOME A MISSED SHOT WITH TWO HANDS TO TRIGGER A HUGE OVATION FROM THE CROWD AND THE KU BENCH LATE IN SATURDAY'S 88-51 VICTORY AGAINST OHIO UNIVERSITY IN THE SPRINT CENTER.

"I was running back, being the trailer, I saw it come off, and I'm like, 'I hope it comes off my way,' and it did, and I put it back home," Aldrich said. "It was fun. It was just exhilarating doing that in front of the TV cameras with all my friends and family watching back home."

Aldrich, a 6-foot-11, 245-pound native of Bloomington, Minn., has been scoring in a variety of ways as the second big man off the bench. Short bank shots, hook shots, put-backs off the glass, dunks.

In the past three games, against Eastern Washington, DePaul and Ohio, Aldrich has played a combined 33 minutes, time enough to total 18 points, 15 rebounds and five blocked shots.

Aldrich has played as many as 15 minutes in four games, but it has been during his practice time, he said, that he has progressed the most. Seniors Darnell Jackson and Sasha Kaun and sophomore Darrell Arthur have gotten most of the post-player minutes, but Aldrich looks more comfortable all the time.

"I'd love to be playing major minutes and whatnot, but I love Sasha, Darnell and Shady, so if they're doing their thing, I'm happy, and I'm cheering them on," Aldrich said.

Playing daily against the three players he mentioned has sped up Aldrich's improvement.

"We all hit each other in practice," Jackson said. "There's no brother-in-law ball. We don't play soft with each other. We do that, and nobody is going to get better. If you get hit in the mouth with an elbow, it's, 'You all right?' 'Yeah.' Then we just keep playing through it. It was real tough on Cole at the beginning because he wasn't used to playing against big guys in high school. He has a long way to go, but he's learning. He asks questions every day."

Aldrich's role will expand with the departure of Kaun, Jackson and perhaps Arthur, but nobody's waiting until next season for him to be a significant contributor.

"Cole is going to bring a lot to the table this year, especially when Big 12 ball comes," Jackson said. "I see it. The coaches see it. Everybody sees it. He's getting better every day." **KU**

Thad Allender

TYREL REED

[AKA] **TYREEZY/T SQUEEZE**
[POSITION] **GUARD**
[YEAR] **FRESHMAN**
[NUMBER] **14**

A lifelong fan of Kansas basketball and a native of Burlington, Reed is not used to losing. In high school, he was the star, and Burlington went 95-4 during his career. During his first season at Kansas, the team went 37-3 and won a national title. The difference, of course, was that Reed mostly watched for Kansas. Early in the season, Reed displayed a nice three-point shooting touch and moved the ball with confidence. His development was stunted when he sprained one ankle, and then another. Struggling to keep up defensively at times, Reed never regained a role, but gained valuable practice experience. »

Full Name: Tyrel Reed
Birthplace: Burlington, Kansas
Hometown: Burlington, Kansas
High School: Burlington
Major: Physical Therapy

HEIGHT	WEIGHT	PTS
6' 3"	185	47
FG %	3PT %	FT %
.514	.458	.000
PPG	ASSISTS	STEALS
2.0	21	7

Nick Krug

IS REED WHAT KU NEEDS?

FEBRUARY 22, 2008 / BY TOM KEEGAN

AMES, IOWA — KANSAS UNIVERSITY FRESHMAN GUARD TYREL REED PLAYED 99 VARSITY BASKETBALL GAMES FOR BURLINGTON HIGH. HE LOST FOUR.

"Pretty much devastated," he said of how he felt after each of those losses. "You never expect you're going to lose. It was tough. I wasn't used to losing. I don't think anyone was."

The fact he used the word "devastated" to describe a loss suggests he just might be what this team in a funk needs at the moment in the way of urgency.

Limited to 21 minutes in Big 12 games, Reed has a chance at significant playing time tonight against Iowa State for all the wrong reasons. Rodrick Stewart is in Seattle, attending his brother's funeral. Sherron Collins, battling a painful knee bruise, is considered probable.

Reed's possible chance comes two days after Kansas received a commitment from another point guard, 6-foot-3 Tyrone Appleton of Midland (Texas) Community College. Looking to the future, Reed's fight for a spot in the playing rotation is getting crowded. Wisely, Reed does his best to keep his mind from straying too far forward.

"I'm more focused on this season right now, wanting to get better," Reed said. "We have a great opportunity to be great this year, and hopefully, we can fulfill what we expect of ourselves. Next year, I mean, that's next year. I guess I'll think about that more when it comes."

It must be more difficult than it sounds, given that he will be a sophomore and Sherron Collins and Appleton will be juniors, Mario Chalmers a senior.

"It's hard not to think about next year, but in the whole scheme of things, this year's way more important than next year right now," Reed said. "You've got to live in the moment. I know we've got some great recruits coming in, and I look forward to still being here."

Desire and an efficient approach to the game are not the issues with Reed. Quickness and experience against big-time competition have been his biggest hurdles, as well as nagging ankle injuries he said he has recovered from completely.

It's all new to him, even playing with a big man, something he said he never did in high school.

His biggest adjustment?

"I'd say defensively, playing against great guards every game, the speed of it and the physicality," said Reed, who gets his best training going against teammates Collins, Chalmers and Russell Robinson. "I know I have to get a lot better at that. That's something I'm going to be working on this year and throughout the summer."

Offensively, he has posted positive statistics, shooting .458 on three-pointers and totaling 17 assists and just three turnovers.

Reed's biggest contribution in a Big 12 game came in Allen Fieldhouse against Colorado when he scored six points in eight minutes, hitting a pair of three-pointers. In the next game, against a more athletic Oklahoma State team, Reed did not get off the bench. If he's frustrated over a lack of playing time, he hides it well.

"I've known that Kansas is a much bigger thing than one person," Reed said. "That's how I've always felt growing up. I've just loved Kansas basketball. I didn't care if I was the main player or anything like that, and I don't think anyone feels like that on our team. We're just going to play as a unit and represent Kansas on the front of our uniforms." KU

Nick Krug

"You've got to live in the moment. I know we've got some great recruits coming in, and I look forward to still being here."

FRESHMAN REED HEALTHY — AND PLAYING LIKE IT

JANUARY 2, 2008 / BY GARY BEDORE

TYREL REED, WHO HAD MISSED FOUR OF SEVEN GAMES PRIMARILY BECAUSE OF ANKLE SPRAINS, HAD HIS BEST GAME IN FIVE WEEKS SATURDAY AGAINST YALE.

The 6-foot-3, 185-pound Kansas University freshman from Burlington scored eight points off 3-of-3 shooting — including a pair of threes — and had a steal while playing 10 minutes of the Jayhawks' 86-53 victory over the Bulldogs.

It was by far Reed's best personal performance since his eight-point, five-assist, 21-minute outing against Northern Arizona on Nov. 21.

"To be candid, Tyrel since he turned his ankle has not played as well or as confidently as he did before," KU coach Bill Self said. "It was good to see him make shots, get the lid off so he could get his confidence.

"He's a good player. We told him that (day before Yale game), but he hasn't played with the same confidence as before he got hurt. A lot of that is, he puts pressure on himself. He played very well, as evidenced by scoring eight points on three shots."

Reed was caught under Darnell Jackson and twisted his right ankle in the closing seconds of the first half of KU's overtime victory over Arizona on Nov. 25.

He missed two games, then sprained the other ankle in his return game — a solid three-rebound, three-assist, two-point, 15-minute outing against Eastern Washington on Dec. 5.

Reed since then missed two games and played 14 minutes total against Ohio and Miami of Ohio, missing four shots, including three threes leading up to the Yale game.

"Coach knows I'm a good player," Reed said, asked about Self's words of encouragement. "He knows I need to go out there and play the game and not worry about it, stop thinking."

What was the difference against Yale?

"The injuries have finally gone away. I think I was more relaxed. I've been kind of tense and not really going out and having fun," Reed said. "I tried to do a better job of not thinking so much."

For the year, Reed has made 14 of 27 shots for 51.9 percent, including nine of 19 threes for 47.4 percent. He has 12 assists against just two turnovers.

"Just being a good teammate," Reed said, asked his goals for the remainder of the season. "I am not worried about playing or anything like that. I know it'll all come in time. I am just going out there trying to win every game. That's a team goal.

"I'll do whatever coach wants. Coach wants me to be ready."

Self is convinced Reed will impact the KU program.

"A lot of guys say they want it. Tyrel decided he wanted it and went after it," Self said of the small-school player earning a major-college scholarship. "He drove from Burlington to Lawrence three days a week to work with a strength-and-conditioning coach the last four years. He shot every day at 6 a.m. during his high school career — every day. If you want it that bad, you make it happen. He's made it happen, and he has ability, above everything else."

The No. 3-rated Jayhawks' next game will be against Boston College at 11 a.m. Saturday at Conte Forum in Chestnut Hill, Mass. The Eagles take a 9-2 record into tonight's home game against Longwood. KU

CONNER TEAHAN

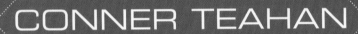

[AKA] **CT**
[POSITION] **GUARD**
[YEAR] **FRESHMAN**
[NUMBER] **2**

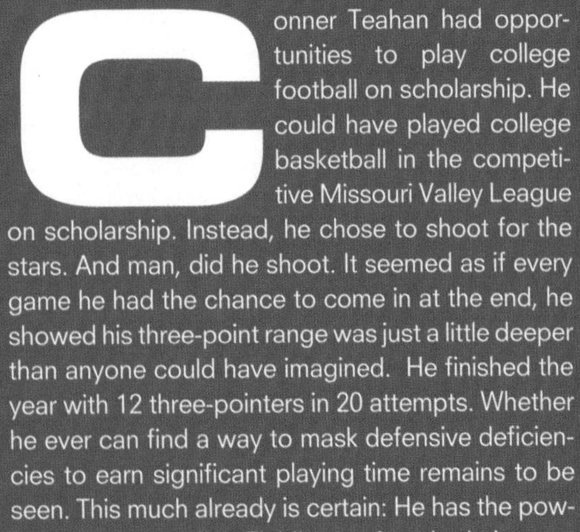

Conner Teahan had opportunities to play college football on scholarship. He could have played college basketball in the competitive Missouri Valley League on scholarship. Instead, he chose to shoot for the stars. And man, did he shoot. It seemed as if every game he had the chance to come in at the end, he showed his three-point range was just a little deeper than anyone could have imagined. He finished the year with 12 three-pointers in 20 attempts. Whether he ever can find a way to mask defensive deficiencies to earn significant playing time remains to be seen. This much already is certain: He has the power to keep the Allen Fieldhouse fans in their seats until the final buzzer, no matter the score. »

Full Name: Conner Michael Teahan
Birthplace: Leawood, Kansas
Hometown: Leawood, Kansas
High School: Rockhurst
Major: Undecided

HEIGHT	WEIGHT	PTS
6' 5"	205	46
FG %	3PT %	FT %
.593	.600	1.000
PPG	ASSISTS	STEALS
2.2	6	2

Nick Krug

TEAHAN ON TOP OF HEAP

NOVEMBER 29, 2007 / BY TOM KEEGAN

THE TOUGHEST THING ABOUT GARBAGE TIME DURING A COLLEGE BASKETBALL GAME IS WATCHING THE PATRONIZING CHEERS FOR WALK-ONS AND THE GUT-BUSTING BY THE REGULARS THAT TAKES PLACE ON THE BENCH WHEN ONE OF THE NON-SCHOLARSHIP PLAYERS SCORES.

Why laugh at them? If they weren't positively influencing the program in some way, they wouldn't get a uniform.

The best thing about watching garbage time of Kansas University basketball games against ridiculously overmatched opponents, such as Florida Atlantic University, which played the tomato can Wednesday night in Allen Fieldhouse?

Watching Conner Teahan shoot from beyond NBA three-point range. Between the time he misfired his first three-point shot as a college player and the time his rainbow from the left corner just in front of the KU bench glanced off the rim with 15 seconds left in KU's 87-49 victory against FAU, here was the result of every three-pointer Teahan took: Swish. Swish. Swish. Swish. Swish. Swish. Swish. Swish. The freshman from Rockhurst High in Kansas City, Mo., made eight in a row.

Named Mr. Show-Me Basketball by the Missouri Coaches Association, Teahan turned down basketball scholarship offers from several Missouri Valley schools and a football scholarship from Tulsa University.

He came to KU and knew he would have to do more than shoot his way into contention for a spot in the rotation. He has a long way to go defensively and as a ballhandler before he gets the meaningful minutes. Meanwhile, he has been so entertaining firing up shots late in games that it pays to stay until the end of blowouts.

Teahan played nine minutes and scored nine points against FAU, and his points-per-minute rate actually dropped. For the season, he has scored 26 points in 23 minutes.

"He can shoot," coach Bill Self said of Teahan. "Good God he can shoot. And he's not scared to shoot it. Defensively and some other things he's got to tighten up a lot. Usually, in tight games I play the guys I trust the most, and I have to develop that with all our young guys. That's not a knock on him or Cole (Aldrich) or Tyrel (Reed). That's just the way it is."

Reed and Aldrich will get crunch-time minutes before Teahan, but that doesn't mean Teahan always will be a garbage-time sensation.

"I predict that he'll be part of our rotation in some way, shape or form during his time here, I just don't know when that time will be," Self said.

Teahan averaged 25 points a game during his senior year in high school.

"I knew coming in here I could shoot, and I think they knew that, too, but I have so many more aspects of my game I need to work on," Teahan said. "Sooner or later, I think I'll get used to the speed of the game. Defensively is where I need to improve the most, defensively and ballhandling. If I can improve on those things, I think I'll break into the lineup sooner or later."

He has become a late-game favorite for all the right reasons, not in a patronizing way.

"I kind of zone out before I shoot it and while I shoot it, but once it goes in and the crowd goes crazy, you can definitely feel it, and it kind of picks you up," Teahan said.

It's mutual. He sends them home smiling, not laughing. KU

BIG XII TOURNAMENT

KU VS. NEBRASKA

KU VS. TEXAS A&M

KU VS. TEXAS

/ BY GARY BEDORE

Kansas University's basketball team discovered a new home away from home during the 2007-08 season in brand-new Sprint Center, a short hop, skip and jump from Allen Fieldhouse.

The Jayhawks, who pounded Ohio University by 37 points in their first-ever game in the downtown Kansas City building on Dec. 15, opened their long postseason run with three convincing victories in the 2008 Big 12 Tournament from March 14-16.

A pair of career-best efforts from Brandon Rush and Mario Chalmers propelled the Jayhawks to their to third consecutive league tourney title, lighting up KC's Power and Light District.

After falling asleep in a 64-54 first-round victory over Nebraska, Rush exploded for a personal-best 28 points in KU's 77-71 semifinal win over Texas A&M. Chalmers then followed with his career-high 30 points in a thrilling 84-74 title win over Texas. »

Nick Krug

Nick Krug

Following the UT game, coach Bill Self stood off to the side and watched with pride as his Big 12 champions played with, and posed with, the league tournament title trophy high atop a podium.

"That was a heck of a basketball game ... what an unbelievable game," Self exclaimed after shaking hands with his assistant coaches after the final horn.

The win not only avenged a regular-season loss to the Longhorns, but gave the Jayhawks a No. 1 seed in the NCAA Tournament's Midwest Regional over Texas (28-6), which fell to a No. 2 seed in the South.

"That's about as well-played a game as you can get," Self said. "It was one of the best games I've been a part of. It was humbling sitting on the sidelines watching those guys play." »

Nick Krug

TEXAS
22
KANSAS
4
KANSAS
Sprint

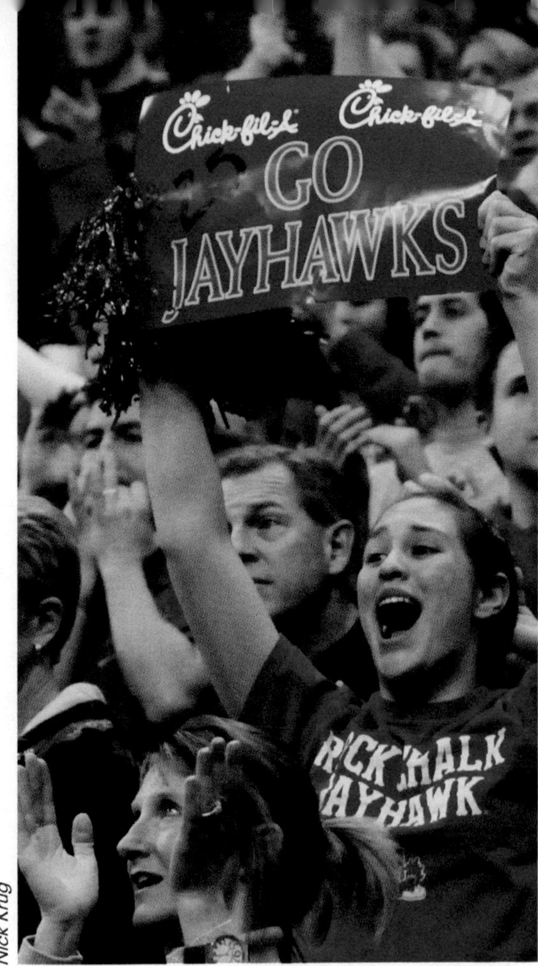

Nick Krug

A pair of career-best efforts from Brandon Rush and Mario Chalmers propelled the Jayhawks to their to third consecutive league tourney title, lighting up KC's Power and Light District.

The 2008 title game proved to be an old-fashioned shootout. KU hit a Big 12 tourney-record 15 threes - one off the school record set against Baylor in 2005 - in 25 tries to the Longhorns' 12 threes in 28 attempts.

Chalmers, who made the all-tournament team, hit eight three-pointers in 12 tries, good for a career-high 30 points, while tourney MVP Rush canned six treys in nine tries and scored 19 points.

Chalmers - his 30 points were most by a Jayhawk since Julian Wright's 33 versus Missouri in 2006-07 - scored KU's first eight points of the final half. His back-to-back threes turned a 49-47 deficit into a 53-49 lead with 13:51 to play. »

Nick Krug

ÖLEVIA
TOYOTA
QuikTrip
TIME WARNERCABLE
KANSAS
Sprint
NCAA BB
www.big12sports.com
Kansas city
Sprint
Center

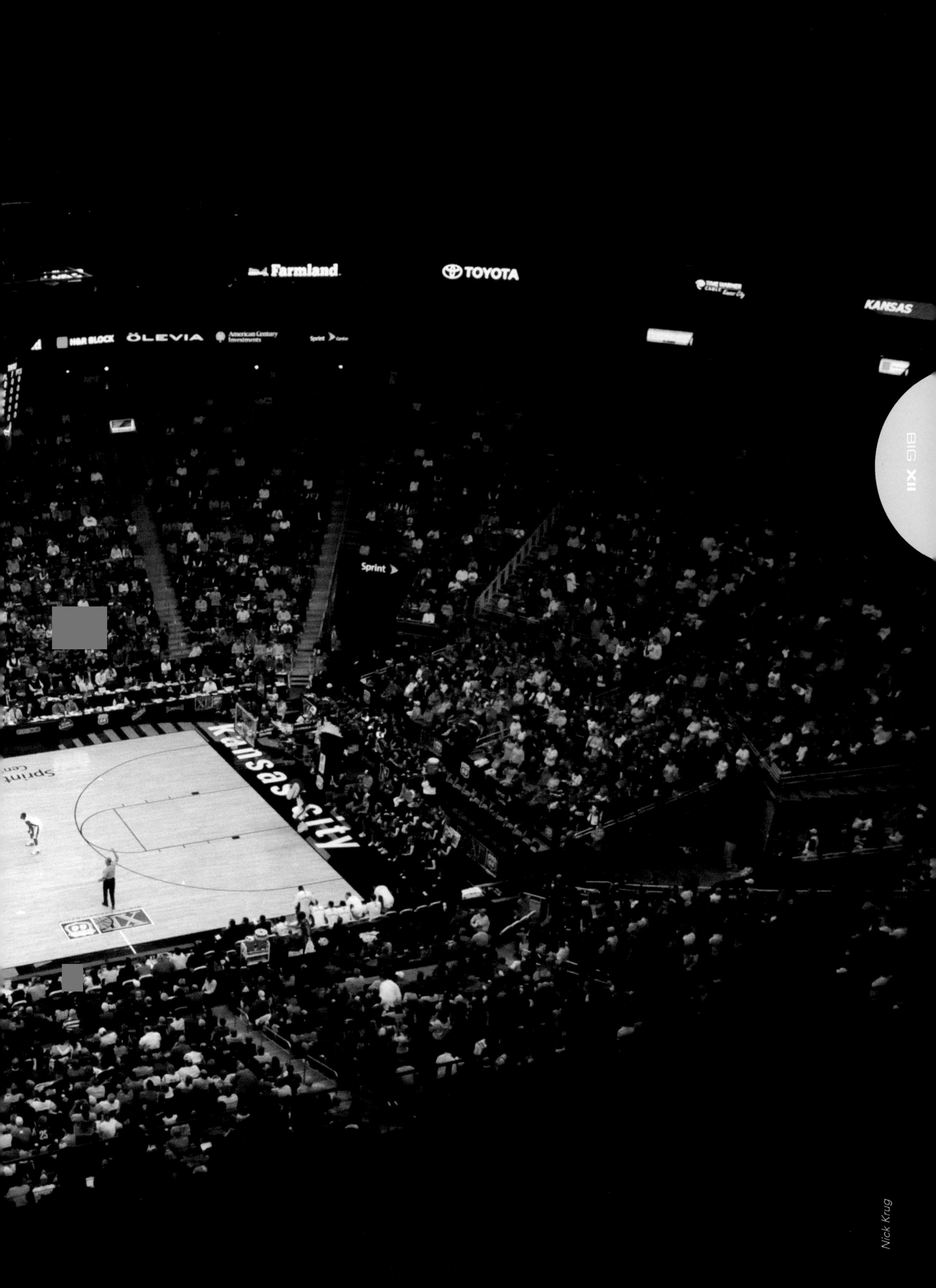

Nick Krug

BIG XII

Nick Krug

The Anchorage, Alaska native also iced a three to stretch a 72-71 lead to four points with 1:51 remaining.

And he stole a D.J. Augustin pass, was fouled and hit two free throws at :40.1, giving the Jayhawks an insurmountable 80-73 advantage.

"It's the greatest game of my college career," Chalmers said after tying Billy Thomas (eight versus Texas in 1998) for second-most threes in a game in KU history, trailing only Terry Brown's 11 against North Carolina State in 1991.

In the 77-71 semifinal win over A&M, Rush in front of a batch of family and friends scored 28 points - 20 in the second half. »

Nick Krug

"That was a heck of a basketball game ... what an unbelievable game," Self exclaimed.

Rush hit nine of 13 shots, including five of eight threes, and also was 5-for-5 from the free-throw line. He played strong defense on A&M forward Josh Carter, who bricked eight of 10 shots and scored just five points.

He didn't hesitate when asked if it was the best of his 102 games in a KU jersey.

"By far," Rush said.

"I couldn't miss so I kept shooting and shooting, and they kept falling and falling."

The 64-54 win over Nebraska in Round One would be called "ugly." »

"It's the greatest game of my college career," Chalmers said.

BIG XII

Nick Krug

KU trailed NU by nine points with 1:30 left in the first half and by five (27-22) at halftime.

KU's sleepy play - the Jayhawks had 12 turnovers against just five assists the first half - had Self seething at the break.

"He was really frustrated with the way we were playing," KU senior forward Darnell Jackson said, crediting a cutting halftime speech as the main reason for KU's come-from-behind victory.

"He didn't freak out at all. The only thing he said was, 'Do you want to go home? Or do you want to advance?' We answered him with our play the second half."

The Jayhawks went on an early 14-2 run to turn a 29-24 deficit into a 38-31 lead six minutes into the half.

In all, the tournament had a little bit of everything, well preparing KU for the NCAAs. KU

Nick Krug

RED**SCARE**

KU forced to rally past Cornhuskers

MARCH 15, 2008 / BY GARY BEDORE

Kansas City, Mo. — Maybe it's because Kansas University's basketball players had pummeled Nebraska by 35 points at home and 21 on the road this season and expected to pound NU again without breaking a sweat.

Or maybe playing 40 miles from Allen Fieldhouse gave the heavily favored Jayhawks a false sense of security.

Whatever the reasons, No. 2-seeded KU trailed No. 7-seed Nebraska by nine points with 1:30 left in the first half and by five at halftime of a Big 12 tournament quarterfinal clash Friday night at Sprint Center.

KU's sloppy play — the Jayhawks had 12 turnovers against just five assists the first half — had KU coach Bill Self seething at the break.

"He was really frustrated with the way we were playing," KU senior forward Darnell Jackson said, crediting a cutting halftime speech as the main reason for KU's 64-54 come-from-behind victory.

"He didn't freak out at all. The only thing he said was, 'Do you want to go home? Or do you want to advance?' We answered him with our play the second half."

The Jayhawks (29-3) went on an early 14-2 run to turn a 29-24 deficit into a 38-31 lead six minutes into the half. »

Nick Krug

Brandon Rush, who scored three points the first half, had six points, while Darrell Arthur, who scored two points the first half, had four in the surge.

Rush said Self gave him a piece of his mind in the locker room for not being aggressive.

"I really deserved it. I played crappy the first half. I can't even say the words he said," Rush said with a smile. "He wasn't loud. He was moving around and talking. He said, 'We've got to pick up the intensity, energy, quit committing so many turnovers.'"

"He said we had to play better. We were flat. We didn't come ready to play," noted sophomore guard Sherron Collins, who had seven second-half points.

Obviously concerned his team came out with so little energy, Self is hoping for focus from the start in today's 3:20 p.m., semifinal game against Texas A&M — a 63-60 winner over Kansas State on Friday.

"I will be real candid. I was very disappointed in our team in the first half," Self said. "I was disappointed how we got frustrated. I was disappointed in our energy level. Not that we weren't trying. We played tight. When you play tight, you don't play with as much energy.

"The thing I was most disappointed in ... we are athletic enough we should be a great loose-ball team, and they beat us to the loose balls. At halftime, we didn't talk about X's and O's. We talked about getting back to who we are: 'If it means as much to you as I think it does you'll play better.' And they performed pretty well the second half, especially starting out."

Self does understand — sort of — how a team like KU could be a bit off in Round One of the conference tourney.

"It's a shame you have to get on guys to get 'em to play like that," Self said. "But to be honest, how many teams struggle as a higher seed in the first round of a tournament against a team that won yesterday? It happens all over the country."

KU's coach wasn't particularly alarmed at the off nights of any individual players, like Arthur, who had six points off 1-of-4 shooting with five rebounds in 24 minutes.

"He just didn't have a good night," Self said. "He played better the second half. He needs to be a guy to get you 15, 20 (points) a night. Tonight he had six. He wasn't a presence like he's capable of being, but he'd been pretty good lately."

KU had just three double-figure scorers. Collins led the way with 13, and Jackson and Chalmers had 12 apiece.

"We have to play better than that. We will play better that," Jackson said defiantly. KU

Nick Krug

KANSAS	MIN	FG	FGA	3P	3PA	FT	FTA	OR	DR	TOT	A	PF	ST	TO	BL	PTS
Darrell Arthur	24	1	4	0	0	4	4	2	3	5	1	4	0	4	1	6
Darnell Jackson	24	4	7	0	0	4	8	3	6	9	1	3	3	0	1	12
Russell Robinson	31	0	3	0	3	3	4	1	3	4	5	1	2	1	0	3
Mario Chalmers	37	3	6	1	2	5	7	1	4	5	5	1	3	6	3	12
Brandon Rush	35	3	10	2	5	1	1	4	1	5	0	1	1	4	2	9
Sherron Collins	22	4	6	1	2	4	5	1	0	1	1	4	1	3	0	13
Rodrick Stewart	2	0	0	0	0	0	0	0	0	0	0	0	0	0	0	0
Sasha Kaun	23	4	5	0	0	1	2	1	2	3	0	2	0	0	0	9
Cole Aldrich	2	0	0	0	0	0	0	0	1	1	0	2	0	0	0	0
TEAM	0	0	0	0	0	0	0	1	0	1	0	0	0	0	0	0
TEAM TOTALS	200	19	41	4	12	22	31	14	20	34	13	18	10	18	7	64

PERCENTAGES FG: 46.3% 3PT: 33.3% FT: 71%

NEBRASKA	MIN	FG	FGA	3P	3PA	FT	FTA	OR	DR	TOT	A	PF	ST	TO	BL	PTS
Aleks Maric	32	5	8	0	0	0	0	4	3	7	2	4	2	6	3	10
Sek Henry	21	1	7	0	3	2	2	1	4	5	1	4	2	4	0	4
Steve Harley	36	1	9	1	4	0	0	2	1	3	1	0	0	1	0	3
Ade Dagunduro	25	5	8	2	3	1	2	1	2	3	3	3	3	2	1	13
Ryan Anderson	18	1	4	1	4	0	0	1	1	2	1	4	1	0	0	3
Jay-R Strowbridge	20	3	6	2	4	0	0	0	0	0	2	2	0	1	0	8
Cookie Miller	19	0	1	0	0	1	3	0	1	1	0	1	1	1	0	1
Paul Velander	19	3	6	3	6	3	3	0	0	0	1	4	1	0	0	12
Chris Balham	9	0	1	0	0	0	0	1	0	1	0	1	0	1	0	0
Cole Salomon	1	0	0	0	0	0	0	0	0	0	0	0	0	0	0	0
TEAM	0	0	0	0	0	0	0	2	0	2	0	0	0	1	0	0
TEAM TOTALS	200	19	50	9	24	7	10	12	12	24	11	23	10	17	4	54

PERCENTAGES FG: 52.7% 3PT: 25% FT: 93.3%

TEAM	1	2	SCORE
Kansas	22	42	64
Nebraska	27	27	54

BIG XII

RUSH REVERSAL

Guard's career game puts KU in finale

MARCH 16, 2008 / BY GARY BEDORE

BIG XII

KU VS. NEBRASKA

KU VS. TEXAS A&M

KU VS. TEXAS

Kansas City, Mo. — Sure, he was happy Kansas University's basketball team won the game.

But Brandon Rush also was upset — and a little embarrassed — after missing seven of 10 shots and committing four turnovers in Friday's Big 12 tournament quarterfinal victory over Nebraska.

"I played terrible yesterday," Rush said of his nine-point, five-rebound effort in the Sprint Center building located just a few blocks from his Kansas City home.

"I wanted to come out today and show everybody what I can do."

What the 6-foot-6 junior did Saturday in front of a batch of family and friends was score a career-high 28 points — 20 in the second half — of the Jayhawks' pulsating 77-71 semifinal victory over Texas A&M.

Rush hit nine of 13 shots, including five of eight threes, and also was 5-for-5 from the free-throw line. He had just two rebounds, but played strong defense on A&M forward Josh Carter, who bricked eight of 10 shots and scored just five points.

He didn't hesitate when asked if it was the best of his 102 games in a KU jersey.

"By far," Rush said.

"I couldn't miss so I kept shooting and shooting, and they kept falling and falling. I'd rather have it in the fieldhouse," he added of his career-best performance. "I didn't play well there at times this year. It feels good to get my career high here, though. It feels good to be in Kansas City and put on a good show."

Rush, who was aggressive in calling for the basketball, sank six of eight shots the second half, including three of five three-pointers.

His two free throws and a three-pointer from his favorite spot — the corner — boosted a 65-63 lead to seven points at 3:53.

"It's the hottest I've ever seen him," said senior guard Russell Robinson, who had one key bucket himself — a driving layup that stretched a 73-71 lead to four points at :31. Rush concluded the scoring with a pair of free throws at 6.4 seconds. »

TEXAS A&M
30
Nick Krug

"It's as focused as I've seen him play in a very long time. He knocked down shot after shot, and it wasn't all in one bunch," Robinson added.

KU coach Bill Self, who throughout the course of this and the past two seasons often has had to remind Rush to be aggressive, marveled at the silky-smooth player's effort the second half.

"I thought Brandon was as good today as I've ever seen him," said Self, who ran some plays specifically designed for Rush — the same guy who made just two of nine shots and had three turnovers in last Saturday's 72-55 victory at Texas A&M.

"The thing I'm most proud of ... Brandon didn't play at all yesterday. For him to come back from that I think is a good sign for him. He needs to have some breakout games when it counts the most. Certainly this is one of those type of games."

In adding that Rush (his previous career-high was 24 points three different times) looked like an "NBA guard today," Self said: "If he keeps playing like this or close to it, then I can't imagine this wouldn't be very impressive for a lot of people (scouts) down the road."

Rush nodded in agreement when asked if his performance was one that probably would impress NBA talent evaluators.

"I played good defense, didn't turn it over much (once) slashed to the hole and went to the free-throw line," he said. "I showed I can do more than shoot.

"I'm not worrying about that," he added of NBA talk. "We're trying to win the Big 12 championship, make the Final Four, win a (national) championship."

Thanks in large part to Rush, as well as Robinson (seven assists), Darnell Jackson (14 points, four boards) and Mario Chalmers (five assists, three steals), the Jayhawks advanced to today's 2 p.m. title game against Texas.

KU and the Longhorns tied for the Big 12 regular-season crown at 13-3.

UT stopped KU, 72-69, on Feb. 11 in Austin.

"I wanted another shot at Texas so we can really see who is the best team in the league," Rush said.

KU has beaten Texas in the past two Big 12 title games — 88-84 in overtime last year in Oklahoma City and 80-68 in 2006 in Dallas.

"We definitely want to win it. We want to give our seniors something special. It'd be my third time to win, too," Rush said.

A victory also might give the winner a No. 1 seed in the NCAA Tournament. Tennessee's loss to Arkansas on Saturday might open a slot for the KU-UT victor.

"Maybe," Rush said. "It'd be good if that happened, too. Right now we just want to win the game, win the championship for our seniors." KU

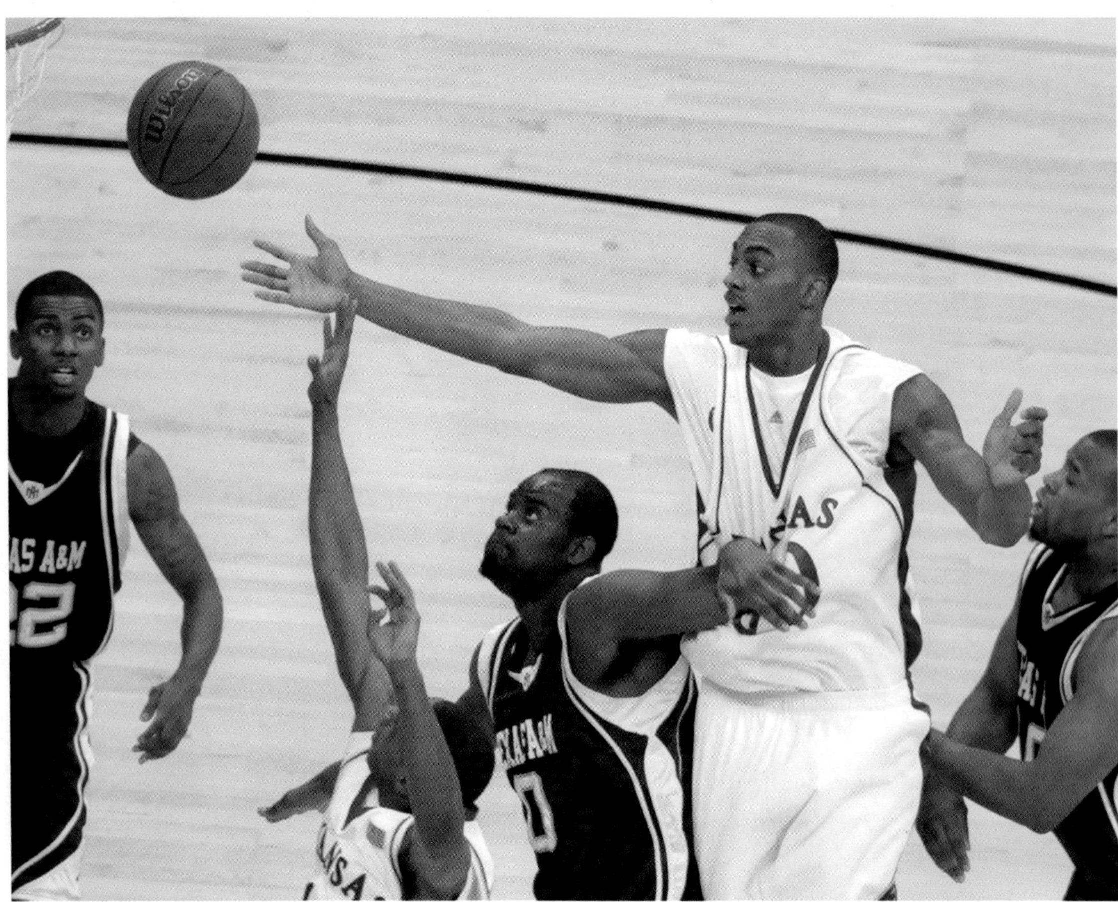

Nick Krug

KANSAS	MIN	FG	FGA	3P	3PA	FT	FTA	OR	DR	TOT	A	PF	ST	TO	BL	PTS
Darrell Arthur	23	3	7	0	0	1	2	2	5	7	0	3	0	2	1	7
Darnell Jackson	27	5	8	0	0	4	6	2	2	4	0	3	1	0	1	14
Russell Robinson	26	2	4	0	1	0	0	1	0	1	7	1	2	1	1	4
Mario Chalmers	30	2	5	0	2	0	1	0	3	3	5	1	3	1	0	4
Brandon Rush	36	9	13	5	8	5	5	1	1	2	1	1	1	1	2	28
Sherron Collins	30	3	8	1	2	2	2	0	2	2	4	1	1	0	0	9
Sasha Kaun	18	1	3	0	0	3	4	1	1	2	0	3	0	1	1	5
Cole Aldrich	10	3	4	0	0	0	0	1	1	2	0	1	1	1	0	6
TEAM	0	0	0	0	0	0	0	0	2	2	0	0	0	0	0	0
TEAM TOTALS	200	28	52	6	13	15	20	8	17	25	17	14	9	7	6	77

PERCENTAGES FG: 53.8% 3PT: 46.2% FT: 75%

TEXAS A&M	MIN	FG	FGA	3P	3PA	FT	FTA	OR	DR	TOT	A	PF	ST	TO	BL	PTS
Bryan Davis	31	5	7	1	1	5	9	4	3	7	0	1	0	2	0	16
Josh Carter	30	2	10	1	8	0	0	1	2	3	3	1	0	0	0	5
Joseph Jones	30	6	10	2	2	0	0	2	1	3	2	3	0	0	1	14
Donald Sloan	12	0	1	0	1	0	0	0	2	2	2	1	1	4	0	0
Dominique Kirk	36	4	11	2	7	2	2	1	3	4	7	3	0	3	0	12
Derrick Roland	18	3	5	1	3	0	0	0	0	0	0	0	0	1	0	7
B.J. Holmes	5	0	2	0	1	0	0	0	2	2	0	0	0	1	0	0
DeAndre Jordan	4	0	0	0	0	1	2	0	0	0	0	3	0	1	0	1
Beau Muhlbach	19	2	6	2	3	5	5	3	1	4	1	4	0	1	0	11
Chinemelu Elonu	15	2	2	0	0	1	2	2	2	4	0	0	0	0	0	5
TEAM	0	0	0	0	0	0	0	3	3	6	0	0	0	0	0	0
TEAM TOTALS	200	24	54	9	26	14	20	16	19	35	15	16	1	13	1	71

PERCENTAGES FG: 52.7% 3PT: 25% FT: 93.3%

TEAM	1	2	SCORE
Kansas	34	43	77
Texas A&M	34	37	71

Nick Krug

THREE-PEAT

Kansas wins 'a heck of a basketball game'

MARCH 17, 2008 / BY GARY BEDORE

Kansas City, Mo. — Bill Self stood off to the side and watched with pride as his Big 12 champions played with, and posed with, the league tournament title trophy high atop a podium Sunday afternoon at Sprint Center.

"That was a heck of a basketball game ... what an unbelievable game," Self, Kansas University's basketball coach, exclaimed after shaking hands with his assistant coaches following the Jayhawks' thrilling 84-74 victory over Texas.

The win not only avenged a regular-season loss to the Longhorns, but gave the Jayhawks (31-3) a No. 1 seed in the NCAA Tournament's Midwest Regional over UT (28-6), which fell to a No. 2 seed in the South.

KU will meet Portland State in a first-round game at 11:25 a.m. Thursday at Qwest Center in Omaha, Neb.

"That's about as well played a game as you can get," Self said. "It was one of the best games I've been a part of. It was humbling sitting on the sidelines watching those guys play. There were some hard-rocking guys out there today."

The 2008 title game proved to be an old-fashioned shootout.

KU hit a Big 12 tourney-record 15 threes — one off the school record set against Baylor in 2005 — in 25 tries to the Longhorns' 12 threes in 28 attempts.

Junior Mario Chalmers, who made the all-tournament team, hit eight three-pointers in 12 tries, good for a career-high 30 points, while tourney MVP Brandon Rush canned six treys in nine tries and scored 19 points.

Chalmers — his previous career high was 23 points twice — scored 17 points the first half to Rush's 12. Texas' D.J. Augustin answered with 18 points off 7-of-9 shooting (4-for-4 threes), however, and the Longhorns led, 46-45, at the break.

"It is pretty corny, but at halftime I told the team in front of Danny (Manning, assistant coach) ... I said, 'That's probably as good a half of »

KU VS. NEBRASKA

KU VS. TEXAS A&M

KU VS. TEXAS

basketball played in Kansas City since the '88 championship game,'" Self said of a 50-50 halftime score in KU's 83-79 victory over Oklahoma on April 4, 1988, at Kemper Arena.

"I asked Danny, 'What happened the second half of that game?' He said the game slowed down and we guarded. That's what happened today. We defended and rebounded the ball much better the second half and played about as complete a game as we've ever played."

Augustin missed nine shots without a make the final half and scored just two points off free throws. Chalmers and Rush, meanwhile, continued to sizz, scoring 13 and seven respectively.

Chalmers — his 30 points were most by a Jayhawk since Julian Wright's 33 versus Missouri last February — scored KU's first eight points of the final half. His back-to-back threes turned a 49-47 deficit into a 53-49 lead with 13:51 to play.

The Anchorage, Alaska native also iced a three to stretch a 72-71 lead to four points with 1:51 remaining.

And he stole an Augustin pass, was fouled and hit two free throws at :40.1, giving the Jayhawks an insurmountable 80-73 advantage.

He was so good on Sunday that teammate Sherron Collins made sure Chalmers had the ball in his hands as the clock expired.

The sophomore guard, who had seven assists and nine points, hand-delivered the ball to Chalmers, who tossed it high in the air and jumped into Rush's arms at the final horn.

"That's the best game Mario has ever played. I thought he deserved to be the one to end that game. I think it meant a lot to him," said Collins, whose clutch three-pointer with 5:40 left erased a 69-67 deficit.

Chalmers agreed it was his finest performance ... with one stipulation.

"It's the greatest game of my college career," he said after tying Billy Thomas (eight versus Texas in 1998) for second-most threes in a game in KU history, trailing only Terry Brown's 11 against North Carolina State in 1991.

What other game could possibly be better?

"One back in high school," he said with a smile, not providing any specifics.

Chalmers — he said the sprained patellar tendon in his left knee gave him no problems Sunday — certainly impressed his teammates with his performance and demeanor.

Chalmers was trading barbs with the Longhorn guards all day.

"They were talking back to us everytime they'd score," Rush said. "It was going up and down. Somebody gets hot and you're going to talk a little smack. I was hot. 'Rio was hot. 'Rio kept shooting the ball and giving his little 'yap-yap' to everybody. We spun it into a positive that way and got the win."

Thanks in great part to Chalmers. "I've never seen him that hot," Rush said.

Darrell Arthur was dandy with 16 points and nine rebounds. Rush was sensational as well, his 28-point semifinal effort against Texas A&M and 19-point, six-rebound, six-assist outing against UT earning him MVP honors in his hometown.

"It's definitely a special feeling now, having everybody in the city see how I played and getting the MVP," Rush said, noting the Jayhawks do not want to rest after sharing the regular-season title with Texas and winning the postseason event.

"We feel this is the year. We've got to do it. We've got five seniors leaving and some others might be leaving early (for NBA). We've got to make it happen now." KU

Nick Krug

"That's about as well played a game as you can get," Self said. "It was one of the best games I've been a part of. It was humbling sitting on the sidelines watching those guys play. There were some hard-rocking guys out there today."

KANSAS	MIN	FG	FGA	3P	3PA	FT	FTA	OR	DR	TOT	A	PF	ST	TO	BL	PTS
Darrell Arthur	36	6	9	0	0	4	4	1	8	9	2	1	1	0	0	16
Darnell Jackson	17	0	2	0	0	3	5	0	2	2	0	4	0	0	0	3
Russell Robinson	23	0	2	0	1	0	0	0	0	0	3	1	0	1	1	0
Mario Chalmers	35	10	15	8	12	2	2	1	3	4	6	3	2	2	0	30
Brandon Rush	39	6	12	6	9	1	2	3	3	6	6	1	0	4	3	19
Sherron Collins	24	2	8	1	3	4	4	1	4	5	7	2	0	2	0	9
Sasha Kaun	23	2	5	0	0	3	7	2	6	8	1	2	0	0	2	7
Cole Aldrich	3	0	0	0	0	0	0	0	0	0	0	1	0	1	1	0
TEAM	0	0	0	0	0	0	0	2	6	8	0	0	0	0	0	0
TEAM TOTALS	200	26	53	15	25	17	24	10	32	42	25	15	3	10	7	84

PERCENTAGES FG: 49.1% 3PT: 60% FT: 70.8%

TEXAS	MIN	FG	FGA	3P	3PA	FT	FTA	OR	DR	TOT	A	PF	ST	TO	BL	PTS
Damion James	36	5	13	3	5	0	0	0	6	6	2	4	0	1	0	13
Connor Atchley	24	2	6	0	3	3	4	2	3	5	1	4	0	0	1	7
A.J. Abrams	36	6	16	3	11	0	0	2	4	6	1	2	1	1	0	15
D.J. Augustin	40	7	18	4	7	2	2	0	1	1	9	4	0	1	0	20
Justin Mason	38	5	8	2	2	5	6	2	3	5	5	1	1	0	1	17
Alexis Wangmene	10	0	2	0	0	0	0	0	1	1	0	2	0	0	0	0
Ian Mooney	0	0	0	0	0	0	0	0	0	0	0	0	0	0	0	0
Dexter Pittman	13	1	1	0	0	0	0	0	2	2	0	2	0	0	1	2
Clint Chapman	3	0	0	0	0	0	0	0	0	0	0	0	0	0	0	0
TEAM	0	0	0	0	0	0	0	2	1	3	0	0	0	1	0	0
TEAM TOTALS	200	26	64	12	28	10	12	8	21	29	18	19	2	4	3	74

PERCENTAGES FG: 40.6% 3PT: 42.9% FT: 83.3%

TEAM	1	2	SCORE
Kansas	45	39	84
Texas	46	28	74

KU / PORTLAND STATE

KU / UNLV

KU / VILLANOVA

KU / DAVIDSON

KU / N. CAROLINA

KU / MEMPHIS

NCAA TOURNAMENT

/ BY GARY BEDORE

One opponent's shot that missed.

One Mario Chalmers shot that swished.

Those two missiles of April - plus a barrage of baskets against Roy Williams' North Carolina Tar Heels - probably best summarize Kansas University's magical six-game run in the NCAA Tournament.

Davidson overachiever Jason Richards missed a 25-footer over both Chalmers and Sherron Collins at the buzzer as the Jayhawks survived the Cinderella team of the tournament, 59-57, in an Elite Eight thriller in Detroit.

Chalmers - the KU history books will forever reveal - hit a deep three over Memphis' Derrick Rose with two seconds left in regulation, sending one of the most exciting national title games in history into overtime. It was a game the Jayhawks went on to win, 75-68.

Oh yes ... a fired-up KU squad raced to a 40-12 lead in a rousing 84-66 national »

Thad Allender

THE UNIVERSITY OF KANSAS
JAYHAWKS
2008
REGIONAL CHAMPIONS

NCAA **TOURNAMENT**

semifinal win over North Carolina, a team that inched within four points of the Jayhawks before running out of gas late.

KU also toppled Portland State, 85-61, and UNLV, 75-56, in first-and second-round action in Omaha, Neb., and pounded Villanova, 72-57, in the Sweet 16.

Chalmers, KU's junior guard from Alaska, had ice in his veins in hitting the all-important three versus Memphis, one that completed a nine-point comeback in the final 2:12.

"Mario saved us like he always does. He hit the biggest three of his life when we needed it the most. That's why we call him Mr. Clutch," KU's Brandon Rush said. »

Thad Allender

NCAA
NCAA.com
BASKETBALL
BRANDON RUSH
Kansas
RUSSELL ROBINSON
Kansas
DARNELL JACKSON
Kansas
MARIO CHALMERS
Kansas

Thad Allender

Chalmers took the modest approach in discussing the shot heard round the world.

"I had an open look. I had a person in my face. It was just a lucky shot," Chalmers said, adding, "I thought it was going in when it left my hands. It felt pretty good when I released it. I'll let everybody else talk about history. I just think it was a big shot."

KU opened the overtime with baskets by Rush, Darrell Arthur and Darnell Jackson and grabbed a six-point lead halfway through the five-minute session. KU never relinquished the advantage.

The semifinal victory over North Carolina was made possible by KU's early onslaught against former coach Williams and national player of the year Tyler Hansbrough.

"It's the best 15 minutes I've ever had a team play because you're playing the No. 1 (overall) seed in the tournament on the biggest stage," Self said. "I felt instead of having 10 hands out there, we had 14 or 16. Guys were all after every ball." »

Nick Krug

"Mario saved us like he always does. He hit the biggest three of his life when we needed it the most. That's why we call him Mr. Clutch."

- Brandon Rush

KU drilled 16 of its first 23 shots in building the 28-point lead and forced six early turnovers against North Carolina. KU also frustrated junior phenom Hansbrough, who was held to 17 points off 6-of-13 shooting.

"They hit us right between the eyes. They just kept hammering," said Williams, whose eyes moistened during his postgame meeting with the media.

In the Elite Eight, KU trailed Davidson by four points with 8:55 left. Self couldn't breathe a final sigh of relief until after the final possession - 16.1 seconds of agony, in which Davidson and sophomore phenom Stephen Curry (25 points, 9-of-25 shooting, four of 16 threes) had a chance to throw in a last-second three-point shot that would have kept a Final Four off Self's otherwise impeccable resume.

Curry - who had been deemed by many the "face of the NCAA Tournament" - brought the ball up court while being well guarded by Rush. Rush slipped 20 feet from the basket with about 10 seconds left, but received immediate help from Mario Chalmers. »

A confused Curry dished to Richards, whose three was long enough, but off to the side. The final horn sounded just after the miss.

"Trust me, I was on both knees," Self said of his position in front of the bench when Richards, who misfired on four three-point attempts, clanged his final try.

Self didn't say whether he was praying, but did admit, "I think they were on our side tonight," referring jokingly to the basketball gods.

KU's Russell Robinson was pivotal in the Sweet 16 win over Villanova.

He scored 13 points, while Rush contributed seven as the Jayhawks raced to a 26-10 lead. Robinson also made sure 'Nova standout guard Scottie Reynolds (11 points, 4-of-13 shooting) was no factor by hounding him on defense. Reynolds had just six points in 18 minutes the first half as KU blazed to a 41-22 lead.

"I didn't let him get going early," Robinson said. "I tried to take away his offense early."

The first and second round victories were efficient, if not pretty.

KU ran into a scrappy team in UNLV in the second round, and the Rebels trailed by just five points midway through the second half at 46-41. KU's athleticism starred on defense and contributed to UNLV missing 33 of 45 shots overall.

Portland State was overmatched in the opener. The Jayhawks, despite an early wake-up call for the 11:25 a.m. tipoff, started fast and cruised into the second round. KU bolted to a 49-26 lead and never was challenged.

"Coach Self made sure we were ready. He jumped us early this morning. He told us, 'You guys gotta wake up!" KU senior Darnell Jackson said. KU

Nick Krug

KANSAS
15

PSU'S GAMBLE COSTLY

VIKES DARE KU TO SHOOT THREES

MARCH 21, 2008 / BY RYAN WOOD

KU / UNLV

KU / VILLANOVA

KU / DAVIDSON

KU / N. CAROLINA

KU / MEMPHIS

Omaha, Neb. — With such inferior ability, Portland State's basketball players had to focus on one of Kansas University's deadly fists and hope the other one didn't kill them.

Admirable. But the Vikings are dead anyway.

The Jayhawks hit 12 three-pointers in their 85-61 victory over the Vikings, taking advantage of what Portland State gave them while the Vikings sagged to try to neutralize the big men.

Kansas (32-3) was 8-of-13 shooting from beyond the arc in the first half, and it only got uglier from there.

"Our game plan was to focus on the bigs and take our chances on them hitting three-pointers," forward Alex Tiefenthaler said, "even though we knew they were capable of hitting three-pointers."

Portland State (23-10) played zone for a good chunk of the first half, which never works against a team featuring Mario Chalmers, Brandon Rush and Sherron Collins bombing away from 20 feet out. KU's big men got their share, too — 15 offensive rebounds turned into 18 second-chance points, and Darrell Arthur (17) and Darnell Jackson (10) both scored in double figures. »

Thad Allender

NCAA
TOURNAMENT

Portland State, meanwhile, seemed overwhelmed by KU's defensive athleticism early, and it led to forward Kyle Coston chucking desperation three-pointers.

But the Vikings calmed down and scored off cuts and solid assists by point guard Jeremiah Dominguez. At one point, the KU lead was cut to 24-18, and the PSU bench felt good.

Briefly.

"I feel like we have a good team," PSU coach Ken Bone said. "Scott Morrison had a good year. Deonte Huff and Jeremiah Dominguez. But none of those three can take over a game like this for a period of time because (of) Kansas' athleticism and their length." »

Thad Allender

Nick Krug

Thad Allender

Nick Krug

Nowhere was that more obvious than with Dominguez, the Big Sky player of the year who had just three first-half points because he couldn't get open. The 5-foot-6 point guard wasn't nearly as athletic as KU's backcourt, and it took some nifty shots late to get him to a team-high 13 points on the day.

So Portland State's first NCAA Tournament appearance ended about like everyone thought it would. But just minutes after the game, while munching away on lunch in the locker room, several Vikings players already had next year in mind.

"It's definitely an experience I'm going to cherish," said Tiefenthaler, a sophomore who had 10 points. "It's the first for me. Hopefully not the last." KU

TEAM	1	2	SCORE
Kansas	49	36	85
Portland State	26	35	61

KANSAS	MIN	FG	FGA	3P	3PA	FT	FTA	OR	DR	TOT	A	PF	ST	TO	BL	PTS
Darrell Arthur	27	8	10	0	0	1	2	4	3	7	1	2	0	0	0	17
Darnell Jackson	21	3	8	0	0	4	4	3	1	4	2	1	2	0	0	10
Russell Robinson	29	2	5	1	4	0	0	0	1	1	4	2	3	4	1	5
Mario Chalmers	31	6	10	3	6	1	2	0	2	2	4	1	3	0	1	16
Brandon Rush	30	7	17	4	9	0	1	1	5	6	2	2	0	2	0	18
Conner Teahan	2	0	0	0	0	0	0	0	0	0	0	0	0	1	0	0
Sherron Collins	22	3	4	3	4	0	0	1	2	3	5	2	0	1	0	9
Rodrick Stewart	8	1	1	0	0	0	0	1	1	2	0	2	0	2	0	2
Jeremy Case	5	1	2	1	2	0	0	0	0	0	1	0	0	0	0	3
Tyrel Reed	2	0	0	0	0	0	0	0	0	0	1	0	0	0	0	0
Sasha Kaun	12	1	2	0	0	1	6	3	4	7	0	0	0	0	0	3
Cole Aldrich	10	1	2	0	0	0	0	0	2	2	1	3	2	1	1	2
Matt Kleinmann	1	0	0	0	0	0	0	0	2	2	0	0	0	0	0	0
TEAM	0	0	0	0	0	0	0	2	0	2	0	0	0	0	0	0
TEAM TOTALS	200	33	61	12	25	7	15	15	23	38	21	15	10	11	3	85

PERCENTAGES FG: 54.1% 3PT: 48% FT: 46.7%

PORTLAND STATE	MIN	FG	FGA	3P	3PA	FT	FTA	OR	DR	TOT	A	PF	ST	TO	BL	PTS
Kyle Coston	26	2	6	1	4	0	2	4	0	4	2	3	0	2	1	5
Scott Morrison	23	2	5	0	0	0	0	1	3	4	0	1	1	1	1	4
Deonte Huff	25	3	8	0	0	3	4	1	3	4	0	2	3	4	1	9
Andre Murray	29	1	5	1	2	2	2	3	1	4	0	0	1	2	0	5
Jeremiah Dominguez	31	4	10	2	7	1	2	0	2	2	4	1	0	2	0	11
Julius Thomas	7	2	2	0	0	0	0	0	1	1	1	4	1	0	0	4
Mickey Polis	4	1	1	1	1	0	0	0	2	2	1	1	0	2	0	3
Brian Curtis	4	0	2	0	2	0	0	0	0	0	0	0	0	0	0	0
Tyrell Mara	16	2	4	1	3	0	0	1	0	1	0	2	1	1	0	5
Dupree Lucas	20	2	5	1	2	0	0	0	0	0	2	2	1	2	0	5
J.R. Moore	7	0	2	0	0	0	0	0	2	2	1	2	0	0	0	0
Alex Teifenthaler	8	2	5	2	4	4	4	0	1	1	0	0	0	0	0	10
TEAM	0	0	0	0	0	0	0	3	3	6	0	0	0	0	0	0
TEAM TOTALS	200	21	55	9	25	10	14	13	18	31	11	18	8	16	3	61

PERCENTAGES FG: 38.2% 3PT: 36% FT: 71.4%

Nick Krug

MOTOWN BOUND!

JAYHAWKS SECURE SWEET 16 SPOT ON MARCH TO FINAL FOUR

MARCH 23, 2008 / BY RYAN WOOD

KU / PORTLAND STATE

KU / UNLV

KU / VILLANOVA

KU / DAVIDSON

KU / N. CAROLINA

KU / MEMPHIS

Omaha, Neb. — It's time for Motown.

Kansas University's men's basketball team secured its slot in the Sweet 16 on Saturday, outlasting Nevada-Las Vegas, 75-56, in the NCAA Tournament's second round.

Step two is complete. The Jayhawks are done in Omaha and will head to Detroit later this week, where they will play Friday against the winner of today's second-round matchup between Siena and Villanova.

Win two in Motown, and the Final Four is the final stop.

After Saturday's game, KU coach Bill Self strutted by a pack of television cameras following him to the locker room. He shook his head, grinned and said, "Exhale."

Relief sounds about right. Kansas (33-3) ran into a scrappy team in UNLV, and the Runnin' Rebels (27-8) fought back to within five midway through the second half at 46-41.

But KU's strengths won out. The Jayhawks' depth was key with a startling 46 fouls called. KU's athleticism starred on defense and contributed to UNLV missing 33 of 45 shots overall.

In the end, Kansas can exhale. The Jayhawks will play in Michigan for only the third time in their NCAA Tournament history. They lost to Bradley in Auburn Hills, Mich., two years ago and won two in Pontiac, Mich., in 1988 en route to their last national championship.

The similarities between the 1988 run and KU's present quest are well-documented. Now, the 2008 Jayhawks are inching closer and closer.

"It's good to move on," KU guard Mario Chalmers said, "but we still have four more games to go." KU

Nick Krug

KANSAS
15
UNLV
1

NCAA
TOURNAMENT

Nick Krug

Nick Krug

"It's good to move on," KU guard Mario Chalmers said, "but we still have four more games to go."

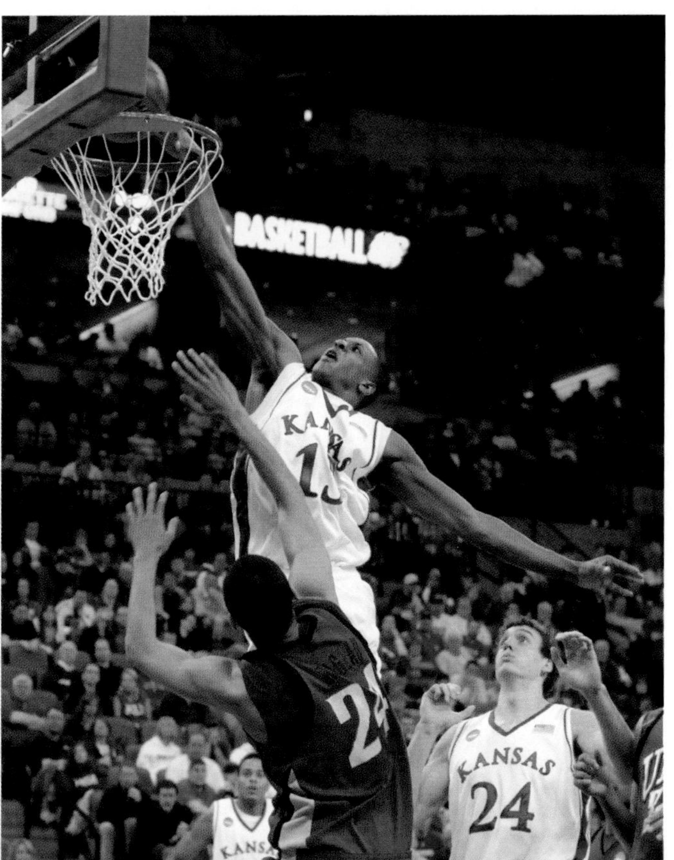

Thad Allender

KANSAS	MIN	FG	FGA	3P	3PA	FT	FTA	OR	DR	TOT	A	PF	ST	TO	BL	PTS
Darrell Arthur	33	4	8	0	0	1	2	1	4	5	1	3	1	4	1	9
Darnell Jackson	25	2	4	0	0	4	6	1	8	9	0	4	0	1	0	8
Russell Robinson	27	4	5	1	2	4	5	1	2	3	2	4	3	1	0	13
Mario Chalmers	34	6	11	2	7	3	5	0	4	4	2	3	2	1	0	17
Brandon Rush	36	5	10	2	3	0	1	0	6	6	3	5	0	1	0	12
Conner Teahan	1	0	0	0	0	0	0	0	0	0	0	0	0	0	0	0
Sherron Collins	27	5	8	0	1	0	0	0	2	2	1	1	0	2	0	10
Jeremy Case	2	0	0	0	0	0	0	0	0	0	0	0	0	0	0	0
Tyrel Reed	1	0	0	0	0	0	0	0	0	0	0	0	1	0	0	0
Sasha Kaun	10	2	3	0	0	0	0	1	1	2	0	4	0	0	0	4
Cole Aldrich	3	1	1	0	0	0	0	0	0	0	0	2	0	0	0	2
Matt Kleinmann	1	0	0	0	0	0	0	0	0	0	0	0	0	0	0	0
TEAM	0	0	0	0	0	0	0	3	2	5	0	0	0	0	0	0
TEAM TOTALS	200	29	50	5	13	12	19	7	29	36	9	26	7	10	1	75

PERCENTAGES FG: 58% 3PT: 38.5% FT: 63.2%

UNLV	MIN	FG	FGA	3P	3PA	FT	FTA	OR	DR	TOT	A	PF	ST	TO	BL	PTS
Corey Bailey	26	0	1	0	0	1	3	1	0	1	1	3	0	1	0	1
Joe Darger	27	3	7	2	6	0	0	0	2	2	1	5	2	3	0	8
Wink Adams	38	5	13	0	3	15	17	1	2	3	3	0	1	0	0	25
Rene Rougeau	28	1	4	0	0	2	2	3	5	8	1	5	2	2	1	4
Curtis Terry	39	3	10	3	8	3	4	0	3	3	0	1	0	2	0	12
Mareceo Rutledge	6	0	2	0	0	0	0	1	1	2	0	0	1	1	0	0
Kendall Wallace	19	0	2	0	1	0	0	0	2	2	0	2	0	1	0	0
Scott Hoffman	1	0	0	0	0	0	0	0	0	0	0	0	0	0	0	0
Troy Cage	1	0	0	0	0	0	0	0	0	0	0	0	0	0	0	0
Matt Shaw	15	0	6	0	4	6	8	3	0	3	0	4	0	0	0	6
TEAM	0	0	0	0	0	0	0	0	2	2	0	0	0	0	0	0
TEAM TOTALS	200	12	45	5	22	27	34	9	17	26	6	20	6	10	1	56

PERCENTAGES FG: 26.7% 3PT: 22.7% FT: 79.4%

Nick Krug

TEAM	1	2	SCORE
Kansas	34	41	75
UNLV	29	27	56

UPSTART VILLANOVA DOOMED BY SLOW START

MARCH 29, 2008 / BY RYAN WOOD

KU / PORTLAND STATE

KU / UNLV

KU / VILLANOVA

KU / DAVIDSON

KU / N. CAROLINA

KU / MEMPHIS

Detroit — Lots of hugs. Lots of silence. And very little that Villanova could've done to prevent it.

A somber Villanova locker room was a foregone conclusion early in Kansas University's 72-57 basketball victory over the Wildcats on Friday. Kansas cruised and advanced to the Midwest Regional final of the NCAA Tournament, while Villanova finished with a 22-13 record.

It was won early, when the Wildcats fell behind, 26-10, fought back, but never cut the deficit to fewer than seven points.

That was that — a 12 seed finally falling after two improbable NCAA Tournament victories.

"For some reason, we're always starting slow," forward Dwayne Anderson said. "We knew it would eventually catch up to us, and tonight it did."

Villanova coach Jay Wright thought his team had a good game plan going into Friday's Sweet 16 showdown at Ford Field. But he said two things turned it to mush right away and made many of the 57,028 fans go home early with the game out of reach: »

Thad Allender

REYNOLDS

• Kansas, which was on fire early, made Villanova's game plan nearly impossible to execute.

• The Wildcats didn't play with enough toughness to hang with the Jayhawks, who improved to 34-3 and will play Davidson on Sunday with a Final Four berth at stake.

"You've got to play great team defense," Wright said. "You can't make mistakes defensively. You just got to play solid because they're going to make some shots.

"And offensively, when you get your looks, it's simple. You got to make your shots. We were 3-of-17 (from three-point range). We had a lot of good looks. You got to be solid." »

Villanova needed good scoring days out of guard Scottie Reynolds and forward Dante Cunningham. Neither came about, with Reynolds scoring just 11 points and Cunningham adding 10.

The Wildcats had five assists to 14 turnovers. They were atrocious from long range and only a little better from inside the three-point arc.

Most of all, they didn't have the talent to keep up with so much going so wrong.

"We had some layups, some threes. Didn't make them," Wright said. "You got to have everything work for you. As I said before this game, we had to play our best game. We didn't tonight.

"I was a little disappointed in our effort, but you've got to give Kansas credit for that." KU

Nick Krug

NCAA TOURNAMENT

It was won early, when the Wildcats fell behind, 26-10, fought back, but never cut the deficit to fewer than seven points.

Nick Krug

TEAM	1	2	SCORE
Kansas	41	31	72
Villanova	22	35	57

NCAA TOURNAMENT

KANSAS	MIN	FG	FGA	3P	3PA	FT	FTA	OR	DR	TOT	A	PF	ST	TO	BL	PTS
Darrell Arthur	24	3	4	0	0	1	2	1	2	3	0	3	0	2	1	7
Darnell Jackson	24	2	5	0	0	0	0	1	5	6	1	1	1	2	0	4
Russell Robinson	33	4	7	3	5	4	4	0	3	3	5	2	1	4	0	15
Mario Chalmers	28	3	7	2	5	6	6	0	3	3	4	4	3	3	0	14
Brandon Rush	28	6	12	2	6	2	2	2	2	4	1	3	1	3	1	16
Conner Teahan	0	0	0	0	0	0	0	0	0	0	0	0	0	0	0	0
Sherron Collins	21	2	5	0	2	0	1	0	2	2	4	3	2	3	0	4
Rodrick Stewart	1	0	0	0	0	0	0	0	0	0	0	0	0	0	0	0
Jeremy Case	9	1	1	1	1	0	0	0	1	1	0	1	0	1	0	3
Tyrel Reed	0	0	0	0	0	0	0	0	0	0	0	0	0	0	0	0
Sasha Kaun	29	3	4	0	0	3	5	1	6	7	0	1	0	0	3	9
Cole Aldrich	3	0	0	0	0	0	0	0	1	1	1	0	0	0	0	0
Matt Kleinmann	0	0	0	0	0	0	0	0	0	0	0	0	0	0	0	0
TEAM	0	0	0	0	0	0	0	2	1	3	0	0	0	0	0	0
TEAM TOTALS	200	24	45	8	19	16	20	7	26	33	16	18	8	18	5	72

PERCENTAGES FG: 53.3% 3PT: 42.1% FT: 80%

VILLANOVA	MIN	FG	FGA	3P	3PA	FT	FTA	OR	DR	TOT	A	PF	ST	TO	BL	PTS
Antonio Pena	12	0	4	0	0	2	2	2	0	2	0	3	0	1	0	2
Dwayne Anderson	30	4	9	0	3	0	1	2	1	3	0	3	4	1	2	8
Dante Cunningham	35	3	8	0	0	4	6	3	4	7	0	3	1	5	0	10
Scottie Reynolds	37	4	13	2	4	1	1	1	1	2	0	2	2	4	0	11
Corey Stokes	22	2	5	1	4	1	2	0	0	0	0	1	0	2	0	6
Jason Colenda	0	0	0	0	0	0	0	0	0	0	0	0	0	0	0	0
Corey Fisher	20	2	8	0	4	2	2	0	0	0	4	3	1	1	0	6
Reggie Redding	19	1	2	0	1	2	4	0	3	3	1	0	2	0	0	4
Shane Clark	25	5	10	0	1	0	0	3	4	7	0	2	0	0	0	10
Frank Tchuisi	0	0	0	0	0	0	0	0	0	0	0	0	0	0	0	0
TEAM	0	0	0	0	0	0	0	4	2	6	0	0	0	0	0	0
TEAM TOTALS	200	21	59	3	17	12	18	15	15	30	5	17	10	14	2	57

PERCENTAGES FG: 35.6% 3PT: 17.6% FT: 66.7%

Thad Allender

DAVIDSON'S
LAST GASP GOES AWRY

MARCH 31, 2008 / BY RYAN WOOD

NCAA TOURNAMENT

KU / UNLV

KU / VILLANOVA

KU / DAVIDSON

KU / N. CAROLINA

KU / MEMPHIS

Detroit — One of college basketball's most lethal shooters didn't get the last chance to kill Kansas University.

Davidson College phenom Stephen Curry had to defer the final shot to teammate Jason Richards. The Wildcats' last gasp banked off the glass to secure KU's 59-57 NCAA Tournament victory Sunday at Ford Field.

Kansas moves on to the Final Four. Davidson ends its season with a 29-7 record, and its 25-game winning streak was snapped.

"I thought it was a good look," Richards said. "Felt like it was in. Unfortunately, it missed."

Curry, who finished with 25 points, unconventionally took the ball up the floor with 16.8 seconds left. It seemed obvious to everybody that the sharpshooter would get the last look to tie or win it for the Wildcats.

"It was designed to be a flat ball screen at the top of the key to get penetration," Curry said. "But they had four guards out there, and they just switched. Kind of defeated the purpose of the play.

"I gave them a pump fake to try to get a look, but I was off balance." »

Thad Allender

DAVIDSON
15
KANSAS
00

KANSAS 35
KANSAS 24
30
KANSAS 25

Thad Allender

Smothered and searching for something, Curry threw it out to Richards at the top of the key. Richards — who finished with seven points and nine assists — chucked up the three-point shot at the buzzer, but banked it off the glass to the left of the rim.

"With the flat ball screen, it's not a guaranteed three," Davidson coach Bob McKillop said. "It gives a lane for penetration or it gives a step back for the three. So we never discussed two or three."

Curry was 9-of-25 shooting on the night and appeared to force some shots in the second half, which is unlike him. Still, he came up big at crucial times, including a three-pointer with 54.5 seconds left that cut the Kansas lead to two.

Thanks to some good defense by the Jayhawks in the closing seconds, it was Curry's final shot of the night. The buzzer-beater instead went to Richards, but his heave at the Final Four came up just short.

"You dream about that stuff when you're a little kid, having the opportunity to win the game and take your team to the Final Four," Richards said. "I had a great look. Steph saw me open at the top of the key. We had a chance to beat Kansas, the No. 1 seed.

"At that point, it seemed like the best shot for us. I felt comfortable taking the shot. Unfortunately, I just missed the shot and fell short." KU

Thad Allender

ARTHUR
00
ROBINSON
3

KANSAS	MIN	FG	FGA	3P	3PA	FT	FTA	OR	DR	TOT	A	PF	ST	TO	BL	PTS
Darrell Arthur	31	3	5	0	0	1	2	1	4	5	1	3	1	1	1	7
Darnell Jackson	23	4	6	0	0	1	4	3	4	7	3	1	1	3	1	9
Russell Robinson	22	0	3	0	2	0	0	0	1	1	1	2	1	4	0	0
Mario Chalmers	33	5	10	3	4	0	0	0	3	3	2	2	2	1	1	13
Brandon Rush	36	4	14	1	5	3	3	2	5	7	2	2	0	1	1	12
Sherron Collins	28	1	8	1	3	2	2	1	2	3	3	2	0	2	0	5
Jeremy Case	2	0	0	0	0	0	0	0	0	0	0	0	0	0	0	0
Sasha Kaun	20	6	6	0	0	1	3	3	3	6	0	3	0	0	1	13
Cole Aldrich	5	0	0	0	0	0	0	0	1	1	0	1	0	1	0	0
TEAM	0	0	0	0	0	0	0	0	5	5	0	0	0	1	0	0
TEAM TOTALS	200	23	52	5	14	8	14	10	28	38	12	16	5	14	5	59

PERCENTAGES FG: 44.2% 3PT: 35.7% FT: 57.1%

NCAA TOURNAMENT

DAVIDSON	MIN	FG	FGA	3P	3PA	FT	FTA	OR	DR	TOT	A	PF	ST	TO	BL	PTS
Thomas Sander	26	3	6	1	1	1	4	0	4	4	2	2	1	0	0	8
Andrew Lovedale	32	3	8	0	0	0	1	2	3	5	1	5	1	0	2	6
Jason Richards	38	3	9	0	4	1	2	0	1	1	9	1	2	4	0	7
Max Paulhus Gosselin	24	0	1	0	1	0	0	0	5	5	2	2	2	2	0	0
Stephen Curry	40	9	25	4	16	3	3	0	4	4	3	1	1	1	0	25
Boris Meno	12	0	0	0	0	0	0	0	1	1	0	1	0	1	0	0
William Archambault	5	0	2	0	1	0	0	0	0	0	0	0	0	0	0	0
Stephen Rossiter	10	0	0	0	0	0	2	2	1	3	0	2	0	1	0	0
Bryant Barr	13	4	6	3	4	0	0	0	1	1	0	1	0	0	0	11
TEAM	0	0	0	0	0	0	0	5	1	6	0	0	0	0	0	0
TEAM TOTALS	200	22	57	8	27	5	12	9	21	30	17	15	7	9	2	57

PERCENTAGES FG: 38.6% 3PT: 29.6% FT: 41.7%

Thad Allender

00.0
WERNER

BRING ON MEMPHIS

KU DOMINATES UNC ON MARCH TO TITLE GAME

APRIL 6, 2008 / BY RYAN WOOD

NCAA
TOURNAMENT

KU / PORTLAND STATE

KU / UNLV

KU / VILLANOVA

KU / DAVIDSON

KU / N. CAROLINA

KU / MEMPHIS

San Antonio — The Rock Chalk chant started with 1:36 remaining, signifying Kansas University's place on the doorstep of a national championship.

KU's men's basketball team beat North Carolina, 84-66, Saturday in a high-energy Final Four showdown, propelling the Jayhawks into Monday's national championship game.

Kansas will play Memphis, another aggressive team that beat UCLA, 78-63, in equally impressive fashion earlier Saturday.

KU's victory in the nightcap demonstrated an almost surreal showing of high and low tides. Kansas led, 40-12, after a furious first-half run, only to see North Carolina storm back and cut KU's lead to four at 54-50 midway through the second half.

Eventually, KU righted the ship and finished on a 30-16 run to secure the victory, led by the 25-point, seven-rebound effort of Brandon Rush.

By the end of the night, the Jayhawks' famous chant was swirling in the Alamodome, as Kansas improved to 36-3 on the season. High-fives and bear hugs lingered in the KU quadrant long after the game had ended.

The Jayhawks will play in the national championship game for the first time since 2003 and will go for their first title since 1988. Tipoff on Monday is set for 8:21 p.m.

Memphis, now 38-1 on the season, is looking for its first national championship with perhaps its best team in school history.

"It's going to be a great matchup," KU sophomore Sherron Collins said.

With everything on the line. KU

Thad Allender

Nick Krug

Thad Allender

NCAA TOURNAMENT

TEAM	1	2	SCORE
Kansas	44	40	84
North Carolina	27	39	66

KANSAS	MIN	FG	FGA	3P	3PA	FT	FTA	OR	DR	TOT	A	PF	ST	TO	BL	PTS
Darrell Arthur	32	3	9	0	0	0	0	0	9	9	2	2	0	3	4	6
Darnell Jackson	17	5	6	0	0	2	2	1	3	4	2	3	2	0	0	12
Russell Robinson	30	2	5	1	4	2	2	0	4	4	4	2	3	1	0	7
Mario Chalmers	31	5	10	1	3	0	2	0	4	4	3	3	3	2	0	11
Brandon Rush	32	11	17	2	7	1	2	3	4	7	2	2	0	3	1	25
Conner Teahan	0	0	0	0	0	0	0	0	0	0	0	0	0	0	0	0
Sherron Collins	30	4	9	1	1	2	2	1	3	4	4	4	1	7	0	11
Jeremy Case	1	0	0	0	0	0	0	0	0	0	0	1	0	0	0	0
Tyrel Reed	0	0	0	0	0	0	0	0	0	0	0	0	0	0	0	0
Sasha Kaun	10	2	4	0	0	0	0	0	0	0	0	3	0	1	0	4
Cole Aldrich	17	2	4	0	0	4	4	4	3	7	0	1	1	2	4	8
Matt Kleinmann	0	0	0	0	0	0	0	0	0	0	0	0	0	0	0	0
TEAM	0	0	0	0	0	0	0	2	1	3	0	0	0	0	0	0
TEAM TOTALS	200	34	64	5	15	11	14	11	31	42	17	21	10	19	9	84

PERCENTAGES FG: 53.1% 3PT: 33.3% FT: 78.6%

NORTH CAROLINA	MIN	FG	FGA	3P	3PA	FT	FTA	OR	DR	TOT	A	PF	ST	TO	BL	PTS
Deon Thompson	25	2	4	0	0	3	4	0	4	4	0	2	0	1	0	7
Tyler Hansbrough	36	6	13	0	1	5	6	6	3	9	1	3	2	3	0	17
Marcus Ginyard	32	0	3	0	2	0	0	1	2	3	2	1	0	1	0	0
Ty Lawson	28	2	8	1	2	4	4	1	2	3	2	1	0	2	0	9
Wayne Ellington	33	8	21	1	9	1	1	2	4	6	0	3	3	3	1	18
Marc Campbell	0	0	0	0	0	0	0	0	0	0	0	0	0	0	0	0
Quentin Thomas	14	0	2	0	0	0	0	0	1	1	2	1	1	1	0	0
Will Graves	3	0	2	0	1	0	0	1	0	1	0	0	0	1	0	0
Danny Green	21	6	13	3	9	0	0	1	4	5	0	3	1	5	1	15
J.B. Tanner	0	0	0	0	0	0	0	0	0	0	0	0	0	0	0	0
Surry Wood	0	0	0	0	0	0	0	0	0	0	0	0	0	0	0	0
Jack Wooten	0	0	0	0	0	0	0	0	0	0	0	0	0	0	0	0
Alex Stepheson	7	0	1	0	0	0	0	0	0	0	0	0	0	1	1	0
Michael Copeland	1	0	0	0	0	0	0	0	0	0	0	0	0	0	0	0
TEAM	0	0	0	0	0	0	0	1	0	1	0	0	0	0	0	0
TEAM TOTALS	200	24	67	5	24	13	15	13	20	33	7	14	7	18	3	66

PERCENTAGES FG: 35.8% 3PT: 20.8% FT: 86.7%

Thad Allender

MARIO AND THE MIRACLE

KU WORKS OVERTIME FOR TITLE

APRIL 8, 2008 / BY RYAN WOOD

San Antonio — The last strand of net was reserved for head coach Bill Self, who ascended the ladder and cleanly snipped it off the rim.

Cheers engulfed the Alamodome. A national title officially was christened.

Kansas University's basketball team won the 2008 NCAA championship, topping Memphis, 75-68 in overtime, in a thrilling title game for the ages Monday.

The Jayhawks (37-3) are champions for the first time since 1988, surviving the 65-team field largely because of defense, determination and timely playmaking.

Kansas outscored Memphis, 12-5, in the overtime, but it was the clutch shooting of Mario Chalmers that instantly became part of Jayhawk lore. Chalmers drilled a game-tying three-pointer with 2.1 seconds left in regulation, tying the score at 63 and giving Kansas five more minutes to take back the game.

"It'll probably be the biggest shot ever made in Kansas history," Self said.

Chalmers had 18 points and was named the Final Four's Most Outstanding Player. Darrell Arthur led Kansas with 20 points and 10 rebounds.

Self was mobbed by well-wishers on the court when the game ended. After struggling to make the Final Four for years, KU's fifth-year head coach got there and came out with two victories.

It was even more rewarding considering Kansas was down nine points with 2:12 to play and improbably came back to win it.

Afterward, Self was beaming — as one might expect from a championship coach.

"It's one thing to win, it's another to win the way we won," Self said. "There's no quit in these guys." KU

Nick Krug

ORAL
ROBERTS
PORTLAND
STATE
PURDUE
00

Nick Krug

"It's one thing to win, it's another to win the way we won," Self said. "There's no quit in these guys."

Nick Krug

CHALMERS
15
2
CHALMERS
15
2

Nick Krug

03.6
Wilson
CHALMERS
15
NCAA
FOUR
SAN ANTONIO

Nick Krug

"It'll probably be the **biggest shot** ever made in Kansas history," **Self said.**

Mike Yoder

TEAM	1	2	OT	SCORE
Kansas	33	30	12	75
Memphis	28	35	5	68

KANSAS	MIN	FG	FGA	3P	3PA	FT	FTA	OR	DR	TOT	A	PF	ST	TO	BL	PTS
Darrell Arthur	35	9	13	0	0	2	2	5	5	10	1	3	1	3	0	20
Darnell Jackson	29	3	4	0	0	2	2	1	7	8	1	1	1	0	0	8
Russell Robinson	20	1	1	0	0	0	0	0	4	4	1	3	1	3	0	2
Mario Chalmers	40	5	13	2	6	6	6	1	2	3	3	3	4	3	0	18
Brandon Rush	42	5	9	0	2	2	3	1	5	6	2	3	1	3	1	12
Sherron Collins	34	4	10	1	4	2	2	0	4	4	6	3	3	4	0	11
Sasha Kaun	21	2	5	0	0	0	0	1	1	2	0	2	0	1	0	4
Cole Aldrich	4	0	0	0	0	0	0	0	0	0	0	0	0	0	0	0
TEAM	0	0	0	0	0	0	0	0	2	2	0	0	0	0	0	0
TEAM TOTALS	225	29	55	3	12	14	15	9	30	39	14	18	11	17	1	75

PERCENTAGES FG: 52.7% 3PT: 25% FT: 93.3%

MEMPHIS	MIN	FG	FGA	3P	3PA	FT	FTA	OR	DR	TOT	A	PF	ST	TO	BL	PTS
Robert Dozier	39	4	11	1	2	2	3	5	5	10	3	2	1	1	1	11
Joey Dorsey	26	3	3	0	0	0	0	1	1	2	1	5	1	1	2	6
Antonio Anderson	42	3	9	2	7	1	3	1	4	5	1	3	4	2	0	9
Chris Douglas-Roberts	42	7	16	2	5	6	9	0	1	1	1	4	1	2	0	22
Derrick Rose	45	7	17	1	6	3	4	2	4	6	8	1	2	5	0	18
Shawn Taggart	24	1	5	0	1	0	0	2	1	3	0	2	1	1	0	2
Willie Kemp	4	0	0	0	0	0	0	0	0	0	0	0	1	1	0	0
Pierre Niles	1	0	0	0	0	0	0	0	0	0	0	0	0	0	0	0
Doneal Mack	2	0	1	0	1	0	0	0	0	0	0	0	0	0	0	0
TEAM	0	0	0	0	0	0	0	0	1	1	0	0	0	0	0	0
TEAM TOTALS	225	25	62	6	22	12	19	11	17	28	14	17	11	13	3	68

PERCENTAGES FG: 40.3% 3PT: 27.3% FT: 63.2%

Nick Krug

Thad Allender

07/08 REGULAR SEASON STATS

THE **STATS**

TEAM	1	2	SCORE
UL-MONROE	35	43	78
KANSAS	50	57	107

DATE: 11/09/2007 LOCATION: ALLEN FIELD HOUSE

PLAYER	MIN	FG	FGA	3P	3PA	FT	FTA	OR	DR	TOT	A	PF	ST	TO	BL	PTS
DARRELL ARTHUR	25	4	12	1	2	2	3	3	3	6	0	1	2	0	0	11
SASHA KAUN	22	4	6	0	0	0	1	2	3	5	1	3	0	1	1	8
RUSSELL ROBINSON	26	3	7	2	4	2	2	1	3	4	3	2	1	2	0	10
SHERRON COLLINS	26	9	13	4	7	0	0	0	0	0	6	2	4	0	0	22
MARIO CHALMERS	26	2	6	1	4	3	4	0	3	3	6	3	3	3	0	8
CONNER TEAHAN	2	0	2	0	1	0	0	0	1	1	0	1	0	0	0	0
RODRICK STEWART	16	1	4	0	1	1	2	1	1	2	8	0	0	2	0	3
JEREMY CASE	9	2	3	1	1	0	0	0	0	0	1	2	1	1	0	5
BRENNAN BECHARD	2	1	1	0	0	0	0	0	0	0	0	0	0	0	0	2
TYREL REED	11	4	5	3	4	0	0	1	0	1	1	1	0	0	0	11
CHASE BUFORD	2	0	0	0	0	0	0	1	0	1	0	1	0	0	0	0
DARNELL JACKSON	18	8	9	0	0	5	5	3	1	4	0	2	4	2	0	21
BRAD WITHERSPOON	2	0	0	0	0	0	0	0	0	0	0	0	0	2	0	0
COLE ALDRICH	10	2	3	0	0	2	2	3	3	6	0	1	0	0	0	6
MATT KLEINMANN	3	0	1	0	0	0	0	0	0	0	0	1	0	0	0	0
BRANDON RUSH	0	0	0	0	0	0	0	0	0	0	0	0	0	0	0	0
TEAM	0	0	0	0	0	0	0	1	1	2	0	0	0	0	0	0
TEAM TOTALS	200	40	72	12	24	15	19	16	19	35	26	20	15	13	1	107
PERCENTAGES		FG: 55.6%			3PT: 50%			FT: 78.9%								

PLAYER	MIN	FG	FGA	3P	3PA	FT	FTA	OR	DR	TOT	A	PF	ST	TO	BL	PTS
AFAM NWEKE	23	1	2	0	0	0	0	1	4	5	2	2	0	0	0	2
BRANDON ROBERTS	28	4	5	1	1	0	0	0	0	0	4	1	0	4	0	9
TONY HOOPER	27	6	11	2	6	5	6	2	2	4	1	4	1	5	0	19
LANCE BRASHER	25	5	10	2	7	0	2	3	2	5	2	4	0	3	0	12
JONAS BROWN	33	3	7	2	4	0	0	1	3	4	4	3	2	4	0	8
RAPHELLE TURNER	17	1	3	0	0	3	4	2	2	4	1	1	2	1	0	5
KENNETH AVERETTE	2	0	0	0	0	2	2	0	0	0	1	0	0	0	0	2
JORDAN PAYNE	30	4	11	2	6	7	8	0	2	2	1	3	3	5	0	17
SEI PAYE	2	0	0	0	0	0	0	0	1	1	0	0	1	0	0	0
MITCHELL HAMPTON	8	1	1	0	0	0	0	0	1	1	0	1	0	1	1	2
DALKY MELENDEZ	5	1	1	0	0	0	1	0	0	0	0	2	0	1	0	2
TEAM	0	0	0	0	0	0	0	1	1	2	0	0	0	0	0	0
TEAM TOTALS	200	26	51	9	24	17	23	10	18	28	16	21	9	24	1	78
PERCENTAGES		FG: 51%			3PT: 37.5%			FT: 73.9%								

TEAM	1	2	SCORE
UMKC	30	32	62
KANSAS	43	42	85

DATE: 11/11/2007 LOCATION: ALLEN FIELD HOUSE

PLAYER	MIN	FG	FGA	3P	3PA	FT	FTA	OR	DR	TOT	A	PF	ST	TO	BL	PTS
DARRELL ARTHUR	27	5	12	0	0	3	5	3	7	10	3	4	3	2	2	13
SASHA KAUN	24	2	2	0	0	6	13	2	1	3	0	2	1	1	4	10
RUSSELL ROBINSON	35	5	8	3	6	2	4	1	2	3	9	3	2	1	0	15
SHERRON COLLINS	29	3	10	0	6	4	4	0	7	7	4	3	2	3	0	10
MARIO CHALMERS	32	8	13	6	9	1	2	0	2	2	6	3	4	2	0	23
RODRICK STEWART	18	4	4	0	0	0	1	2	2	4	1	0	1	3	0	8
JEREMY CASE	1	0	0	0	0	0	0	0	0	0	0	0	0	0	0	0
TYREL REED	9	0	1	0	1	0	0	0	0	0	0	0	1	0	0	0
DARNELL JACKSON	22	3	7	0	0	0	2	3	1	4	1	0	1	0	1	6
COLE ALDRICH	3	0	0	0	0	0	0	0	2	2	0	1	0	2	0	0
CONNER TEAHAN	0	0	0	0	0	0	0	0	0	0	0	0	0	0	0	0
BRENNAN BECHARD	0	0	0	0	0	0	0	0	0	0	0	0	0	0	0	0
CHASE BUFORD	0	0	0	0	0	0	0	0	0	0	0	0	0	0	0	0
BRAD WITHERSPOON	0	0	0	0	0	0	0	0	0	0	0	0	0	0	0	0
MATT KLEINMANN	0	0	0	0	0	0	0	0	0	0	0	0	0	0	0	0
BRANDON RUSH	0	0	0	0	0	0	0	0	0	0	0	0	0	0	0	0
TEAM	0	0	0	0	0	0	0	0	1	1	0	0	0	0	0	0
TEAM TOTALS	200	30	57	9	22	16	31	11	25	36	24	16	15	14	7	85
PERCENTAGES		FG: 52.6%			3PT: 40.9%			FT: 51.6%								

PLAYER	MIN	FG	FGA	3P	3PA	FT	FTA	OR	DR	TOT	A	PF	ST	TO	BL	PTS
ANE BRUMAGIN	22	3	10	2	6	3	4	2	2	4	3	3	2	2	0	11
BRENT STEPHENS	31	5	15	2	7	1	2	0	4	4	1	4	1	3	0	11
BRIAN GETTINGER	8	0	3	0	2	0	0	0	2	2	0	4	0	0	0	0
REGGIE HAMILTON	33	7	9	2	2	0	0	0	2	2	7	1	2	6	0	16
AKEEM HEMINGWAY	31	1	4	0	1	0	0	0	1	1	4	2	0	3	0	2
JAMES HUMPHREY	23	2	4	0	2	0	0	1	6	7	0	2	1	3	1	4
NATHAN BALCH	5	0	0	0	0	0	0	0	0	0	0	0	0	0	0	0
JEREMIAH HARTSOCK	28	6	7	1	2	3	5	2	6	8	1	2	0	3	0	16
ALEX PLEDGER	4	0	0	0	0	0	0	0	1	1	0	2	0	1	0	0
SPENCER JOHNSON	10	1	3	0	1	0	0	0	0	0	0	2	1	0	0	2
JAKUB JURCZAK	5	0	0	0	0	0	0	0	0	0	0	0	0	1	0	0
TEAM	0	0	0	0	0	0	0	2	0	2	0	0	0	0	0	0
TEAM TOTALS	200	25	55	7	23	7	11	7	24	31	16	22	7	22	1	62
PERCENTAGES		FG: 45.5%			3PT: 30.4%			FT: 63.6%								

TEAM	1	2	SCORE
WASHBURN	18	42	60
KANSAS	34	58	92

DATE: 11/15/2007 LOCATION: ALLEN FIELD HOUSE

PLAYER	MIN	FG	FGA	3P	3PA	FT	FTA	OR	DR	TOT	A	PF	ST	TO	BL	PTS
DARRELL ARTHUR	25	4	8	0	0	6	8	0	5	5	0	3	2	1	2	14
SASHA KAUN	12	4	4	0	0	2	6	4	3	7	0	3	0	2	0	10
RUSSELL ROBINSON	27	2	5	1	4	3	5	0	3	3	6	1	1	4	1	8
RODRICK STEWART	19	3	5	1	3	2	4	3	1	4	4	3	1	1	1	9
MARIO CHALMERS	29	4	6	1	3	1	2	0	4	4	5	1	0	0	1	10
CONNER TEAHAN	5	2	2	2	2	2	2	0	0	0	0	2	0	0	1	8
JEREMY CASE	10	1	5	0	3	0	0	0	0	0	3	1	0	3	0	2
BRENNAN BECHARD	2	1	1	1	1	0	0	1	1	2	0	0	0	0	0	3
TYREL REED	14	3	6	2	3	0	0	0	2	2	2	1	1	1	0	8
CHASE BUFORD	2	0	1	0	1	0	0	0	1	1	0	1	0	0	0	0
BRANDON RUSH	12	3	5	1	2	0	1	1	2	3	2	0	1	0	1	7
DARNELL JACKSON	23	4	7	0	0	2	2	5	2	7	0	1	2	2	2	10
BRAD WITHERSPOON	2	0	1	0	1	0	0	0	0	0	0	0	0	0	0	0
COLE ALDRICH	15	1	5	0	0	1	3	2	2	4	0	0	0	0	1	3
MATT KLEINMANN	3	0	0	0	0	0	0	0	0	0	0	0	0	0	0	0
SHERRON COLLINS	0	0	0	0	0	0	0	0	0	0	0	0	0	0	0	0
TEAM	0	0	0	0	0	0	0	1	0	1	0	0	0	0	0	0
TEAM TOTALS	200	32	61	9	23	19	33	17	26	43	22	17	8	14	9	92
PERCENTAGES	FG: 52.5%			3PT: 39.1%		FT: 57.6%										

PLAYER	MIN	FG	FGA	3P	3PA	FT	FTA	OR	DR	TOT	A	PF	ST	TO	BL	PTS
PAUL BYERS	13	1	2	0	1	0	0	1	0	1	0	3	1	2	0	2
DARNELL KIMBLE	18	4	10	1	2	0	0	3	2	5	0	4	0	2	1	9
ANDREW MEILE	25	3	5	1	3	0	0	0	4	4	1	0	0	3	0	7
MARIO SCOTT	24	3	7	0	1	4	6	0	2	2	1	1	5	4	0	10
JAMES WILLIAMS	23	3	11	1	3	4	5	0	2	2	2	2	1	3	0	11
ANGEL SANTIAGO	13	4	6	3	5	0	0	0	0	0	1	2	0	0	0	11
GRANT HARGETT	24	1	7	1	5	0	0	2	2	4	4	1	1	2	0	3
MORIBA DECOTEAU	4	1	1	0	0	0	0	1	0	1	0	1	0	0	0	2
DEI DEI	5	0	1	0	1	0	0	0	1	1	0	2	0	0	0	0
NATE DANIELS	10	0	1	0	1	0	2	0	0	0	1	0	1	1	0	0
BRADY SISK	21	2	7	0	0	1	1	7	1	8	3	4	1	1	0	5
GARRETT LOVE	2	0	1	0	0	0	0	0	0	0	0	1	0	0	0	0
KYLE SNYDER	18	0	2	0	0	0	0	1	7	8	0	3	0	1	1	0
TEAM	0	0	0	0	0	0	0	1	1	2	0	0	0	0	0	0
TEAM TOTALS	200	26	51	9	24	17	23	10	18	28	16	21	9	24	1	78
PERCENTAGES	FG: 51%			3PT: 37.5%		FT: 73.9%										

TEAM	1	2	SCORE
NORTHERN ARIZ	10	36	46
KANSAS	44	43	87

DATE: 11/21/2007 LOCATION: ALLEN FIELD HOUSE

PLAYER	MIN	FG	FGA	3P	3PA	FT	FTA	OR	DR	TOT	A	PF	ST	TO	BL	PTS
DARRELL ARTHUR	24	8	10	0	1	1	2	2	4	6	1	0	0	1	3	17
SASHA KAUN	16	3	3	0	0	1	3	1	2	3	0	2	1	0	3	7
RUSSELL ROBINSON	23	2	6	1	4	0	0	1	2	3	3	0	0	2	0	5
RODRICK STEWART	19	3	3	1	1	1	1	1	0	1	4	2	2	1	0	8
MARIO CHALMERS	20	3	6	0	1	1	1	0	2	2	6	3	3	1	0	7
CONNER TEAHAN	7	3	3	3	3	0	0	0	0	0	1	1	0	0	0	9
JEREMY CASE	9	0	2	0	2	0	0	0	0	0	2	0	0	0	0	0
BRENNAN BECHARD	3	0	1	0	1	0	0	0	0	0	0	0	0	0	0	0
TYREL REED	21	3	4	2	3	0	1	0	1	1	5	0	1	0	0	8
CHASE BUFORD	3	0	2	0	2	0	0	0	0	0	0	1	0	1	0	0
BRANDON RUSH	16	2	5	2	4	0	0	0	2	2	1	1	1	2	1	6
DARNELL JACKSON	15	5	8	1	2	2	2	1	7	8	0	0	0	1	0	13
BRAD WITHERSPOON	2	0	0	0	0	0	0	0	0	0	0	0	0	0	0	0
COLE ALDRICH	17	3	3	0	0	1	4	0	3	3	1	0	2	0	1	7
MATT KLEINMANN	5	0	1	0	0	0	0	2	1	3	1	1	0	0	1	0
SHERRON COLLINS	0	0	0	0	0	0	0	0	0	0	0	0	0	0	0	0
TEAM	0	0	0	0	0	0	0	1	1	2	0	0	0	0	0	0
TEAM TOTALS	200	35	57	10	24	7	14	9	25	34	25	11	10	9	9	87
PERCENTAGES	FG: 61.4%			3PT: 41.7%		FT: 50%										

PLAYER	MIN	FG	FGA	3P	3PA	FT	FTA	OR	DR	TOT	A	PF	ST	TO	BL	PTS
KYLE LANDRY	27	2	8	0	0	0	0	3	2	5	0	4	1	1	0	4
ZARKO COMAGIC	23	2	8	0	1	4	4	2	2	4	0	1	1	4	1	8
MATT JOHNSON	28	2	8	1	4	0	0	0	1	1	2	0	1	4	0	5
NATHAN GEISER	18	2	5	1	4	0	0	0	0	0	0	3	1	1	0	5
JOSH WILSON	26	3	6	2	4	0	0	0	3	3	2	0	0	5	0	8
CAMERON JONES	21	3	7	0	1	2	2	1	2	3	3	1	0	1	0	8
GEORGE SHARP	10	0	2	0	0	0	0	0	0	0	0	1	0	0	0	0
ZACK FILZEN	17	1	3	0	1	0	0	0	1	1	2	1	0	0	0	2
NICK LARSON	17	2	6	2	3	0	0	1	1	2	1	3	1	2	0	6
SHANE JOHANNSEN	13	0	1	0	0	0	0	0	2	2	0	1	1	0	0	0
TEAM	0	0	0	0	0	0	0	5	2	7	0	0	0	0	0	0
TEAM TOTALS	200	17	54	6	18	6	6	12	16	28	10	15	6	18	1	46
PERCENTAGES	FG: 31.5%			3PT: 33.3%		FT: 100%										

TEAM	1	2	OT	SCORE
ARIZONA	40	22	10	72
KANSAS	40	22	14	76

DATE: 11/25/2007 LOCATION: ALLEN FIELD HOUSE

PLAYER	MIN	FG	FGA	3P	3PA	FT	FTA	OR	DR	TOT	A	PF	ST	TO	BL	PTS
DARRELL ARTHUR	34	8	13	0	0	4	6	3	3	6	0	4	0	5	3	20
SASHA KAUN	25	3	5	0	0	0	0	0	2	2	1	2	3	1	2	6
RUSSELL ROBINSON	25	0	3	0	3	2	2	0	0	0	3	4	3	3	0	2
RODRICK STEWART	27	5	8	0	1	3	4	1	5	6	2	3	1	0	0	13
MARIO CHALMERS	37	5	11	0	2	4	6	0	1	1	7	4	3	2	1	14
JEREMY CASE	4	0	0	0	0	0	0	0	0	0	0	0	0	0	0	0
TYREL REED	7	0	1	0	1	0	0	0	0	0	1	0	0	0	0	0
BRANDON RUSH	36	6	12	2	2	3	4	1	7	8	2	0	1	1	0	17
DARNELL JACKSON	29	2	5	0	1	0	0	1	4	5	1	3	0	3	1	4
COLE ALDRICH	1	0	0	0	0	0	0	0	0	0	0	0	0	0	0	0
CONNER TEAHAN	0	0	0	0	0	0	0	0	0	0	0	0	0	0	0	0
BRENNAN BECHARD	0	0	0	0	0	0	0	0	0	0	0	0	0	0	0	0
CHASE BUFORD	0	0	0	0	0	0	0	0	0	0	0	0	0	0	0	0
BRAD WITHERSPOON	0	0	0	0	0	0	0	0	0	0	0	0	0	0	0	0
MATT KLEINMANN	0	0	0	0	0	0	0	0	0	0	0	0	0	0	0	0
SHERRON COLLINS	0	0	0	0	0	0	0	0	0	0	0	0	0	0	0	0
TEAM	0	0	0	0	0	0	0	0	1	1	0	0	0	0	0	0
TEAM TOTALS	225	29	58	2	10	16	22	6	23	29	17	20	11	15	7	76
PERCENTAGES	FG: 50%				3PT: 20%			FT: 72.7%								

PLAYER	MIN	FG	FGA	3P	3PA	FT	FTA	OR	DR	TOT	A	PF	ST	TO	BL	PTS
CHASE BUDINGER	38	10	23	6	12	1	3	1	5	6	1	5	2	5	0	27
JORDAN HILL	24	2	5	0	0	1	2	2	3	5	0	4	0	2	1	5
KIRK WALTERS	19	0	1	0	0	1	4	0	3	3	0	2	1	2	1	1
JERRYD BAYLESS	31	5	9	2	2	7	7	1	2	3	2	2	1	7	0	19
JAWANN MCCLELLAN	33	2	4	2	4	0	0	0	3	3	2	1	1	4	0	6
DANIEL DILLON	2	0	1	0	1	0	0	0	0	0	0	0	0	1	0	0
NIC WISE	32	2	6	0	2	3	4	1	2	3	6	3	0	3	0	7
JAMELLE HORNE	16	2	2	0	0	0	0	2	1	3	0	3	0	0	0	4
BRET BRIELMAIER	30	1	3	0	0	1	1	3	5	8	3	5	0	1	0	3
EAM	0	0	0	0	0	0	0	2	2	4	0	0	0	0	0	0
TEAM TOTALS	225	24	54	10	21	14	21	12	26	38	14	25	5	25	2	72
PERCENTAGES	FG: 44.4%				3PT: 47.6%			FT: 66.7%								

TEAM	1	2	SCORE
FLA ATLANTIC	19	30	49
KANSAS	38	49	87

DATE: 11/28/2007 LOCATION: ALLEN FIELD HOUSE

PLAYER	MIN	FG	FGA	3P	3PA	FT	FTA	OR	DR	TOT	A	PF	ST	TO	BL	PTS
DARRELL ARTHUR	17	6	9	0	1	0	0	0	2	2	2	3	0	1	1	12
DARNELL JACKSON	22	4	5	1	1	4	4	3	1	4	0	3	0	0	2	13
RUSSELL ROBINSON	27	1	4	0	2	1	2	2	3	5	2	1	3	2	0	3
RODRICK STEWART	21	1	4	0	2	1	2	1	0	1	8	0	1	0	1	3
MARIO CHALMERS	25	4	5	3	4	0	0	0	3	3	2	3	0	2	0	11
CONNER TEAHAN	9	3	4	3	4	0	0	0	1	1	1	1	0	1	0	9
JEREMY CASE	15	3	4	1	2	0	0	1	2	3	6	0	0	0	0	7
BRENNAN BECHARD	4	0	1	0	1	1	2	0	1	1	0	1	0	0	0	1
CHASE BUFORD	3	0	2	0	1	0	0	1	0	1	0	0	0	1	0	0
SASHA KAUN	16	3	4	0	0	1	4	0	7	7	0	2	0	1	2	7
BRANDON RUSH	19	6	14	3	8	2	2	0	1	1	0	0	2	0	0	17
BRAD WITHERSPOON	3	0	0	0	0	0	0	1	0	1	1	0	0	0	0	0
COLE ALDRICH	15	2	2	0	0	0	0	1	4	5	0	4	3	2	2	4
MATT KLEINMANN	4	0	0	0	0	0	1	1	0	1	0	1	0	0	0	0
TYREL REED	0	0	0	0	0	0	0	0	0	0	0	0	0	0	0	0
SHERRON COLLINS	0	0	0	0	0	0	0	0	0	0	0	0	0	0	0	0
TEAM	0	0	0	0	0	0	0	0	1	1	0	0	0	0	0	0
TEAM TOTALS	200	33	58	11	26	10	17	11	26	37	22	19	9	10	8	87
PERCENTAGES	FG: 56.9%				3PT: 42.3%			FT: 58.8%								

PLAYER	MIN	FG	FGA	3P	3PA	FT	FTA	OR	DR	TOT	A	PF	ST	TO	BL	PTS
DERRICK SIMMONS	20	1	2	0	0	0	0	0	0	0	1	3	0	2	0	2
JEFF PARMER	26	2	7	1	2	0	0	2	1	3	3	1	2	5	0	5
CARLOS MONROE	30	1	8	0	0	2	8	0	5	5	1	2	1	2	0	4
CARDERRO NWOJI	35	3	10	3	6	5	6	0	5	5	3	2	0	3	0	14
SANCHEZ HUGHLEY	25	5	8	0	2	4	5	3	1	4	0	2	3	2	0	14
ENRIQUE RODRIGUEZ	5	0	0	0	0	0	0	0	1	1	0	0	0	1	0	0
XAVIER PERKINS	21	0	5	0	0	1	2	3	2	5	0	2	1	2	1	1
SEAN ALARCON	18	2	4	1	1	0	0	0	0	0	0	2	0	0	0	5
BRETT ROYSTER	20	2	7	0	0	0	0	3	2	5	0	3	1	1	3	4
TEAM	0	0	0	0	0	0	0	2	2	4	0	0	0	0	0	0
TEAM TOTALS	200	16	51	5	11	12	21	13	19	32	8	17	8	18	4	49
PERCENTAGES	FG: 31.4%				3PT: 45.5%			FT: 57.1%								

TEAM	1	2	SCORE
USC	27	28	55
KANSAS	25	34	59

DATE: 12/2/2007 LOCATION: LOS ANGELES, CA

PLAYER	MIN	FG	FGA	3P	3PA	FT	FTA	OR	DR	TOT	A	PF	ST	TO	BL	PTS
DARRELL ARTHUR	25	5	11	0	1	0	2	4	4	8	0	5	1	5	0	10
DARNELL JACKSON	33	4	10	0	0	1	2	4	9	13	2	2	0	1	1	9
RUSSELL ROBINSON	33	2	7	1	4	0	0	0	0	0	1	3	2	4	0	5
RODRICK STEWART	29	2	7	0	1	0	0	3	4	7	1	1	0	5	0	4
MARIO CHALMERS	33	6	11	3	6	5	8	2	5	7	0	3	3	5	0	20
SASHA KAUN	19	1	1	0	0	3	4	0	2	2	0	4	0	1	1	5
BRANDON RUSH	26	2	11	0	5	2	2	1	2	3	2	0	1	1	0	6
COLE ALDRICH	2	0	0	0	0	0	0	0	0	0	0	2	0	0	0	0
JEREMY CASE	0	0	0	0	0	0	0	0	0	0	0	0	0	0	0	0
TYREL REED	0	0	0	0	0	0	0	0	0	0	0	0	0	0	0	0
CONNER TEAHAN	0	0	0	0	0	0	0	0	0	0	0	0	0	0	0	0
BRENNAN BECHARD	0	0	0	0	0	0	0	0	0	0	0	0	0	0	0	0
CHASE BUFORD	0	0	0	0	0	0	0	0	0	0	0	0	0	0	0	0
BRAD WITHERSPOON	0	0	0	0	0	0	0	0	0	0	0	0	0	0	0	0
MATT KLEINMANN	0	0	0	0	0	0	0	0	0	0	0	0	0	0	0	0
SHERRON COLLINS	0	0	0	0	0	0	0	0	0	0	0	0	0	0	0	0
TEAM	0	0	0	0	0	0	0	0	2	2	0	0	0	0	0	0
TEAM TOTALS	200	22	58	4	17	11	18	14	28	42	6	20	7	22	2	59
PERCENTAGES		FG: 37.9%			3PT: 23.5%			FT: 61.1%								

PLAYER	MIN	FG	FGA	3P	3PA	FT	FTA	OR	DR	TOT	A	PF	ST	TO	BL	PTS
DAVON JEFFERSON	36	6	11	0	0	5	7	0	3	3	1	3	1	3	0	17
DWIGHT LEWIS	25	2	3	0	1	0	0	0	0	0	3	3	0	5	0	4
TAJ GIBSON	25	1	4	0	0	0	3	1	4	5	0	5	0	2	0	2
DANIEL HACKETT	40	4	9	2	2	1	2	0	6	6	2	1	2	3	1	11
O.J. MAYO	40	6	21	3	11	4	6	1	4	5	2	3	3	5	0	19
ANGELO JOHNSON	15	0	1	0	1	0	0	0	1	1	2	2	0	0	0	0
KEITH WILKINSON	10	1	2	0	0	0	0	1	1	2	1	2	0	0	0	2
ROUSEAN CROMWELL	0	0	0	0	0	0	0	0	0	0	0	1	0	0	0	0
KASEY CUNNINGHAM	9	0	1	0	0	0	0	2	1	3	0	0	0	0	0	0
TEAM	0	0	0	0	0	0	0	1	4	5	0	0	0	0	0	0
TEAM TOTALS	200	20	52	5	15	10	18	6	24	30	11	20	6	18	1	55
PERCENTAGES		FG: 38.5%			3PT: 33.3%			FT: 55.6%								

TEAM	1	2	SCORE
EASTERN WASH	23	24	47
KANSAS	37	48	85

DATE: 12/5/2007 LOCATION: ALLEN FIELD HOUSE

PLAYER	MIN	FG	FGA	3P	3PA	FT	FTA	OR	DR	TOT	A	PF	ST	TO	BL	PTS
DARRELL ARTHUR	25	7	12	1	1	0	0	4	2	6	0	2	2	2	1	15
DARNELL JACKSON	25	6	8	0	0	5	8	3	6	9	0	3	1	4	0	17
RUSSELL ROBINSON	26	1	4	1	3	6	6	0	2	2	3	1	3	0	2	9
RODRICK STEWART	17	2	6	1	1	2	2	1	2	3	2	1	0	1	0	7
MARIO CHALMERS	27	2	7	0	4	2	2	1	2	3	8	3	6	1	0	6
CONNER TEAHAN	2	2	2	1	1	0	0	0	0	0	0	0	0	0	0	5
JEREMY CASE	8	0	2	0	1	0	0	0	0	0	1	1	1	0	0	0
BRENNAN BECHARD	1	0	1	0	1	0	0	0	0	0	1	0	0	0	0	0
TYREL REED	15	1	3	0	2	0	0	0	3	3	3	0	0	0	0	2
CHASE BUFORD	1	0	1	0	0	0	0	0	0	0	0	0	0	0	0	0
SASHA KAUN	12	2	3	0	0	3	4	2	1	3	2	2	1	1	1	7
BRANDON RUSH	22	4	11	1	3	0	1	3	7	10	0	1	1	2	0	9
BRAD WITHERSPOON	1	0	0	0	0	0	0	0	0	0	0	0	0	0	0	0
COLE ALDRICH	15	2	4	0	0	2	2	1	6	7	0	1	0	0	3	6
MATT KLEINMANN	3	1	2	0	0	0	0	2	0	2	0	0	0	0	0	2
SHERRON COLLINS	0	0	0	0	0	0	0	0	0	0	0	0	0	0	0	0
TEAM	0	0	0	0	0	0	0	0	0	0	0	0	0	0	0	0
TEAM TOTALS	200	30	66	5	17	20	25	17	31	48	20	15	15	11	7	85
PERCENTAGES		FG: 45.5%			3PT: 29.4%			FT: 80%								

PLAYER	MIN	FG	FGA	3P	3PA	FT	FTA	OR	DR	TOT	A	PF	ST	TO	BL	PTS
MATT BRUNELL	23	1	5	1	4	0	0	0	2	2	1	3	0	2	0	3
KELLEN WILLIAMS	35	5	9	3	6	0	0	2	9	11	0	1	1	2	1	13
MARCUS HINTON	14	0	4	0	1	0	0	0	1	1	0	1	0	2	0	0
GARY GIBSON	19	2	4	1	2	0	0	1	1	2	1	5	1	2	0	5
TREY GROSS	33	1	7	0	3	0	0	0	0	0	1	2	1	5	0	2
ADRIS DELEON	25	8	11	3	5	5	5	0	1	1	2	1	0	4	0	24
MILAN STANOJEVIC	29	0	6	0	5	0	0	0	2	2	0	1	3	2	0	0
JACK LOOFBURROW	1	0	0	0	0	0	0	0	0	0	0	0	0	0	0	0
BRANDON MOORE	21	0	6	0	0	0	2	2	6	8	0	3	0	2	1	0
TEAM	0	0	0	0	0	0	0	0	0	0	0	0	0	1	0	0
TEAM TOTALS	200	17	52	8	26	5	7	5	22	27	5	17	6	22	2	47
PERCENTAGES		FG: 32.7%			3PT: 30.8%			FT: 71.4%								

TEAM	1	2	SCORE
DEPAUL	22	44	66
KANSAS	39	45	84

DATE: 12/15/2007 LOCATION: KANSAS CITY, MO

PLAYER	MIN	FG	FGA	3P	3PA	FT	FTA	OR	DR	TOT	A	PF	ST	TO	BL	PTS
DARRELL ARTHUR	22	6	12	0	0	1	1	0	0	0	1	3	0	2	2	13
DARNELL JACKSON	22	4	6	0	0	0	1	4	4	8	2	4	0	3	0	8
RUSSELL ROBINSON	31	2	3	0	1	3	4	1	0	1	9	2	2	1	1	7
RODRICK STEWART	17	1	3	0	0	2	2	1	1	2	1	2	1	1	0	4
MARIO CHALMERS	32	5	9	2	4	0	0	1	8	9	7	3	7	2	0	12
CONNER TEAHAN	4	0	1	0	1	0	0	0	1	1	1	0	0	0	0	0
SHERRON COLLINS	13	2	4	2	3	0	1	0	0	0	1	1	0	1	0	6
JEREMY CASE	4	0	1	0	1	0	0	0	1	1	1	0	0	0	0	0
BRENNAN BECHARD	1	0	0	0	0	0	0	0	0	0	0	0	0	0	0	0
CHASE BUFORD	1	0	0	0	0	0	0	0	0	0	0	0	0	0	0	0
SASHA KAUN	15	6	7	0	0	3	4	3	2	5	1	2	0	2	2	15
BRANDON RUSH	29	5	14	3	7	0	0	1	1	2	1	1	1	1	1	13
BRAD WITHERSPOON	1	0	1	0	1	0	0	0	0	0	0	0	0	0	0	0
COLE ALDRICH	8	3	4	0	0	0	0	1	2	3	0	1	0	1	2	6
TYREL REED	0	0	0	0	0	0	0	0	0	0	0	0	0	0	0	0
MATT KLEINMANN	0	0	0	0	0	0	0	0	0	0	0	0	0	0	0	0
TEAM	0	0	0	0	0	0	0	1	1	2	0	0	0	0	0	0
TEAM TOTALS	200	34	65	7	18	9	13	13	21	34	25	19	11	14	8	84
PERCENTAGES		FG: 52.3%			3PT: 38.9%			FT: 69.2%								

PLAYER	MIN	FG	FGA	3P	3PA	FT	FTA	OR	DR	TOT	A	PF	ST	TO	BL	PTS
DAR TUCKER	30	7	18	2	6	2	2	5	6	11	2	3	1	1	1	18
KARRON CLARKE	28	3	6	2	4	2	2	0	4	4	0	3	1	1	0	10
MAC KOSHWAL	33	3	7	1	1	2	8	4	6	10	0	2	1	4	1	9
JABARI CURRIE	21	1	5	0	2	1	2	0	0	0	4	1	1	4	0	3
DRAELON BURNS	24	3	11	2	4	2	4	2	0	2	2	2	0	5	0	10
MICHAEL BIZOUKAS	4	1	1	0	0	0	0	0	1	1	1	0	0	1	0	2
CLIFF CLINKSCALES	18	2	3	2	3	0	0	0	0	0	1	0	0	1	0	6
ADAM HANDLER	2	0	2	0	1	0	0	1	0	1	0	0	0	0	1	0
WILL WALKER	20	2	3	1	2	1	2	0	1	1	1	1	1	2	0	6
MATIJA POSCIC	20	1	3	0	0	0	0	1	1	2	1	4	0	2	0	2
EAM	0	0	0	0	0	0	0	5	2	7	0	0	0	1	0	0
TEAM TOTALS	200	23	59	10	23	10	20	18	21	39	12	16	5	22	3	66
PERCENTAGES		FG: 39%			3PT: 43.5%			FT: 50%								

TEAM	1	2	SCORE
OHIO	20	31	51
KANSAS	46	42	88

DATE: 12/15/2007 LOCATION: KANSAS CITY, MO

PLAYER	MIN	FG	FGA	3P	3PA	FT	FTA	OR	DR	TOT	A	PF	ST	TO	BL	PTS
DARRELL ARTHUR	25	5	10	0	1	4	6	3	5	8	0	2	1	2	2	14
DARNELL JACKSON	23	5	5	0	0	1	2	1	7	8	2	2	0	1	0	11
RUSSELL ROBINSON	25	2	3	2	3	0	0	0	3	3	11	0	3	2	1	6
MARIO CHALMERS	25	7	9	3	4	0	0	0	3	3	5	0	4	2	0	17
BRANDON RUSH	25	4	11	3	7	2	2	2	1	3	3	0	0	1	1	13
CONNER TEAHAN	3	1	1	0	0	0	0	0	2	2	0	0	1	1	0	2
SHERRON COLLINS	21	2	6	2	5	0	2	1	2	3	0	1	1	2	0	6
RODRICK STEWART	10	0	0	0	0	2	2	1	1	2	0	0	0	3	0	2
JEREMY CASE	6	1	4	1	3	0	0	0	0	0	3	1	2	0	0	3
TYREL REED	8	0	3	0	2	0	0	0	0	0	0	0	0	1	0	0
SASHA KAUN	17	4	6	0	0	0	1	4	3	7	0	2	0	0	2	8
COLE ALDRICH	10	3	4	0	0	0	0	2	2	4	0	2	0	1	1	6
MATT KLEINMANN	2	0	0	0	0	0	0	0	0	0	0	0	0	0	0	0
BRENNAN BECHARD	0	0	0	0	0	0	0	0	0	0	0	0	0	0	0	0
CHASE BUFORD	0	0	0	0	0	0	0	0	0	0	0	0	0	0	0	0
BRAD WITHERSPOON	0	0	0	0	0	0	0	0	0	0	0	0	0	0	0	0
TEAM	0	0	0	0	0	0	0	0	3	3	0	0	0	0	0	0
TEAM TOTALS	200	34	62	11	25	9	15	14	32	46	24	10	12	16	7	88
PERCENTAGES		FG: 54.8%			3PT: 44%			FT: 60%								

PLAYER	MIN	FG	FGA	3P	3PA	FT	FTA	OR	DR	TOT	A	PF	ST	TO	BL	PTS
LEON WILLIAMS	32	3	8	0	0	3	4	5	6	11	2	4	1	2	0	9
JUSTIN ORR	21	3	6	1	3	0	0	1	1	2	1	0	0	3	0	7
JEROME TILLMAN	30	2	12	1	4	2	2	2	4	6	1	3	0	0	0	7
MICHAEL ALLEN	30	1	5	1	3	1	2	1	2	3	2	3	1	1	0	4
ADAM (BUBBA) WALTHER	25	2	8	2	8	2	2	0	1	1	3	0	3	3	0	8
DEVAUGHN WASHINGTON	3	0	0	0	0	0	0	0	0	0	0	0	0	0	0	0
BERT WHITTINGTON IV	17	4	10	2	4	0	0	0	0	0	0	0	2	4	0	10
KENNETH VAN KEMPEN	16	0	2	0	0	1	2	1	0	1	0	3	1	1	0	1
ALLEN HESTER	13	0	5	0	3	0	0	0	1	1	0	0	1	1	0	0
TOMMY FREEMAN	13	2	4	1	3	0	0	0	0	0	0	0	1	2	0	5
TEAM	0	0	0	0	0	0	0	1	1	2	0	0	0	0	0	0
TEAM TOTALS	200	17	60	8	28	9	12	11	16	27	9	13	10	17	0	51
PERCENTAGES		FG: 28.3%			3PT: 28.6%			FT: 75%								

TEAM	1	2	SCORE
GEORGIA TECH	29	37	66
KANSAS	36	35	71

DATE: 12/18/2007 LOCATION: ATLANTA, GA

PLAYER	MIN	FG	FGA	3P	3PA	FT	FTA	OR	DR	TOT	A	PF	ST	TO	BL	PTS
DARRELL ARTHUR	19	3	5	0	0	0	0	1	5	6	0	4	0	2	1	6
DARNELL JACKSON	21	2	3	0	0	0	1	0	2	2	2	5	1	3	0	4
RUSSELL ROBINSON	33	4	8	3	6	6	10	0	1	1	4	2	3	2	0	17
MARIO CHALMERS	33	4	7	1	3	2	3	1	0	1	1	5	1	3	1	11
BRANDON RUSH	29	4	8	1	4	2	2	2	4	6	2	1	0	3	4	11
SHERRON COLLINS	24	4	12	1	4	2	2	0	5	5	3	1	3	4	0	11
RODRICK STEWART	13	2	2	0	0	0	1	1	2	3	1	2	0	0	0	4
SASHA KAUN	26	1	1	0	0	5	6	1	2	3	0	2	0	1	3	7
COLE ALDRICH	2	0	0	0	0	0	0	0	0	0	0	0	0	0	0	0
CONNER TEAHAN	0	0	0	0	0	0	0	0	0	0	0	0	0	0	0	0
JEREMY CASE	0	0	0	0	0	0	0	0	0	0	0	0	0	0	0	0
BRENNAN BECHARD	0	0	0	0	0	0	0	0	0	0	0	0	0	0	0	0
TYREL REED	0	0	0	0	0	0	0	0	0	0	0	0	0	0	0	0
CHASE BUFORD	0	0	0	0	0	0	0	0	0	0	0	0	0	0	0	0
BRAD WITHERSPOON	0	0	0	0	0	0	0	0	0	0	0	0	0	0	0	0
MATT KLEINMANN	0	0	0	0	0	0	0	0	0	0	0	0	0	0	0	0
TEAM	0	0	0	0	0	0	0	0	2	2	0	0	0	0	0	0
TEAM TOTALS	200	24	46	6	17	17	25	6	23	29	13	22	8	18	9	71
PERCENTAGES		FG: 52.2%			3PT: 35.3%			FT: 68%								

PLAYER	MIN	FG	FGA	3P	3PA	FT	FTA	OR	DR	TOT	A	PF	ST	TO	BL	PTS
ANTHONY MORROW	27	4	7	2	4	2	2	3	2	5	2	4	2	1	0	12
GANI LAWAL	14	2	2	0	0	1	1	0	2	2	0	2	0	2	0	5
JEREMIS SMITH	21	1	6	0	0	0	0	4	5	9	2	3	0	3	0	2
LEWIS CLINCH	37	8	16	3	10	3	4	1	1	2	0	3	2	2	0	22
MATT CAUSEY	14	3	4	1	2	2	2	0	1	1	2	4	1	4	0	9
MAURICE MILLER	12	0	1	0	0	0	0	0	1	1	4	0	1	2	0	0
LANCE STORRS	4	0	0	0	0	0	0	0	1	1	0	1	0	0	0	0
D'ANDRE BELL	25	3	4	0	0	1	2	0	1	1	1	2	1	1	0	7
ZACH PEACOCK	27	2	9	1	3	0	0	0	3	3	0	2	0	3	0	5
ALADE AMINU	19	1	5	0	0	2	5	2	4	6	0	1	1	0	0	4
TEAM	0	0	0	0	0	0	0	1	2	3	0	0	0	1	0	0
TEAM TOTALS	200	24	54	7	19	11	16	11	23	34	11	22	8	19	0	66
PERCENTAGES		FG: 44.4%			3PT: 36.8%			FT: 68.8%								

TEAM	1	2	SCORE
MIAMI-OHIO	20	34	54
KANSAS	39	39	78

DATE: 12/28/2007 LOCATION: ALLEN FIELD HOUSE

PLAYER	MIN	FG	FGA	3P	3PA	FT	FTA	OR	DR	TOT	A	PF	ST	TO	BL	PTS
DARRELL ARTHUR	23	7	14	0	1	0	0	4	6	10	0	1	0	1	0	14
DARNELL JACKSON	20	6	7	0	0	2	4	4	4	8	1	2	1	1	2	14
RUSSELL ROBINSON	29	1	5	1	5	0	0	0	1	1	4	2	4	2	0	3
MARIO CHALMERS	24	4	6	2	3	0	0	0	0	0	3	4	3	1	1	10
BRANDON RUSH	27	5	9	0	1	0	0	0	3	3	1	0	0	0	0	10
CONNER TEAHAN	3	1	1	1	1	0	0	0	0	0	0	0	0	0	0	3
SHERRON COLLINS	19	3	4	1	2	1	2	0	3	3	3	1	1	0	0	8
RODRICK STEWART	13	1	2	0	0	0	0	0	1	1	2	0	1	0	0	2
JEREMY CASE	6	1	1	0	0	0	0	0	0	0	1	0	0	0	0	2
BRENNAN BECHARD	1	1	1	1	1	0	0	0	0	0	0	0	0	0	0	3
TYREL REED	6	0	1	0	1	0	0	0	0	0	0	0	0	0	0	0
CHASE BUFORD	1	0	0	0	0	0	0	0	1	1	0	0	0	0	0	0
SASHA KAUN	13	2	4	0	0	1	1	1	0	1	0	3	0	1	0	5
BRAD WITHERSPOON	1	0	0	0	0	0	0	0	0	0	1	0	0	0	0	0
COLE ALDRICH	13	1	2	0	0	2	2	0	3	3	1	0	0	0	1	4
MATT KLEINMANN	1	0	0	0	0	0	0	0	0	0	0	0	0	0	0	0
TEAM	0	0	0	0	0	0	0	0	1	1	0	0	0	0	0	0
TEAM TOTALS	200	33	57	6	15	6	9	9	23	32	17	13	10	6	4	78
PERCENTAGES		FG: 57.9%			3PT: 40%			FT: 66.7%								

PLAYER	MIN	FG	FGA	3P	3PA	FT	FTA	OR	DR	TOT	A	PF	ST	TO	BL	PTS
ERIC POLLITZ	21	1	5	0	1	0	0	1	1	2	1	1	0	1	0	2
TIM POLLITZ	28	5	12	1	1	0	1	2	4	6	3	2	2	2	0	11
ADAM FLETCHER	12	1	2	0	0	0	0	1	1	2	0	4	0	2	0	2
KENNY HAYES	24	3	8	1	3	4	4	1	1	2	1	0	1	4	0	11
ALEX MOOSMANN	22	0	4	0	4	0	0	0	0	0	1	0	0	0	0	0
RODNEY HADDIX	5	1	2	1	1	0	0	0	1	1	0	0	0	0	0	3
TYLER DIERKERS	19	1	2	0	0	0	0	1	1	2	1	2	0	0	0	2
CARL RICHBURG	11	1	3	1	2	0	0	1	0	1	3	0	0	1	0	3
SEAN MOCK	1	0	0	0	0	0	0	0	0	0	0	0	0	0	0	0
NICK WINBUSH	12	3	4	2	2	0	0	0	1	1	2	2	0	0	0	8
DWIGHT MCCOMBS	20	3	5	0	0	0	2	3	3	6	1	0	0	2	0	6
MICHAEL BRAMOS	25	2	5	2	3	0	0	0	2	2	1	0	1	2	1	6
TEAM	0	0	0	0	0	0	0	0	1	1	0	0	0	0	0	0
TEAM TOTALS	200	21	52	8	17	4	7	10	16	26	14	11	4	14	1	54
PERCENTAGES		FG: 40.4%			3PT: 47.1%			FT: 57.1%								

TEAM	1	2	SCORE
YALE	19	34	53
KANSAS	42	44	86

DATE: 12/29/2007 LOCATION: ALLEN FIELD HOUSE

PLAYER	MIN	FG	FGA	3P	3PA	FT	FTA	OR	DR	TOT	A	PF	ST	TO	BL	PTS
DARRELL ARTHUR	22	3	9	0	0	5	7	1	3	4	0	2	1	0	3	11
DARNELL JACKSON	24	9	12	0	0	2	5	3	2	5	2	1	1	0	0	20
RUSSELL ROBINSON	25	2	4	0	1	0	0	0	2	2	5	1	8	2	0	4
MARIO CHALMERS	25	3	5	3	5	2	3	0	1	1	5	2	3	2	1	11
BRANDON RUSH	24	4	9	1	4	1	2	0	2	2	3	1	2	1	0	10
CONNER TEAHAN	3	0	2	0	2	0	0	0	0	0	0	0	0	0	1	0
SHERRON COLLINS	16	3	5	2	3	0	0	0	1	1	2	1	0	4	0	8
RODRICK STEWART	11	2	3	0	0	0	2	1	1	2	0	0	1	1	0	4
JEREMY CASE	5	0	2	0	0	0	0	0	1	1	2	0	0	0	0	0
BRENNAN BECHARD	1	0	1	0	0	0	0	0	0	0	0	0	0	0	0	0
TYREL REED	10	3	3	2	2	0	0	0	0	0	0	1	1	0	0	8
CHASE BUFORD	2	0	1	0	1	0	0	0	1	1	0	0	0	0	0	0
SASHA KAUN	16	2	5	0	0	0	2	0	2	2	0	0	1	1	0	4
BRAD WITHERSPOON	2	0	0	0	0	0	0	0	0	0	0	0	0	0	0	0
COLE ALDRICH	12	2	3	0	0	1	2	4	3	7	0	2	0	2	0	5
MATT KLEINMANN	2	0	0	0	0	1	2	0	1	1	0	0	0	0	0	1
TEAM	0	0	0	0	0	0	0	3	3	6	0	0	0	0	0	0
TEAM TOTALS	200	33	64	8	18	12	25	12	23	35	19	11	18	13	5	86
PERCENTAGES		FG: 51.6%			3PT: 44.4%			FT: 48%								

PLAYER	MIN	FG	FGA	3P	3PA	FT	FTA	OR	DR	TOT	A	PF	ST	TO	BL	PTS
ROSS MORIN	23	1	4	0	1	1	2	0	4	4	1	3	1	5	0	3
MATT KYLE	15	1	4	0	0	0	0	1	5	6	0	5	0	1	1	2
ERIC FLATO	27	3	11	2	9	2	2	0	1	1	0	1	1	3	0	10
NICK HOLMES	18	1	4	1	2	0	0	1	2	3	0	0	1	1	0	3
CALEB HOLMES	21	1	6	0	3	0	0	2	2	4	3	1	0	6	0	2
JOSH DAVIS	4	0	0	0	0	0	0	0	0	0	1	1	0	0	0	0
PORTER BRASWELL	15	5	6	3	3	0	0	0	1	1	1	0	0	4	0	13
TRAVIS PINICK	15	2	5	0	2	1	2	0	2	2	0	1	1	4	0	5
JORDAN GIBSON	17	2	6	0	0	0	0	2	1	3	0	0	0	0	0	4
ALEX ZAMPIER	20	1	5	1	4	1	2	1	2	3	4	2	3	2	1	4
PAUL NELSON	18	2	2	0	0	1	2	2	1	3	0	3	0	0	0	5
GARRETT FIDDLER	4	0	0	0	0	0	0	0	2	2	0	1	0	0	0	0
MICHAEL SANDS	3	1	1	0	0	0	0	0	0	0	1	0	0	0	0	2
TEAM	0	0	0	0	0	0	0	2	2	4	0	0	0	1	0	0
TEAM TOTALS	200	20	54	7	24	6	10	11	25	36	11	18	7	27	2	53
PERCENTAGES		FG: 37%			3PT: 29.2%			FT: 60%								

TEAM	1	2	SCORE
BOSTON COLLEGE	29	31	60
KANSAS	47	38	85

DATE: 1/5/2008 LOCATION: BOSTON, MA

PLAYER	MIN	FG	FGA	3P	3PA	FT	FTA	OR	DR	TOT	A	PF	ST	TO	BL	PTS
DARRELL ARTHUR	24	10	12	0	0	2	2	1	6	7	1	4	0	1	2	22
DARNELL JACKSON	32	9	13	0	0	7	8	3	6	9	1	1	2	1	0	25
RUSSELL ROBINSON	24	1	4	1	2	1	2	1	1	2	5	3	2	3	1	4
MARIO CHALMERS	32	3	8	2	4	0	0	0	1	1	6	1	4	0	0	8
BRANDON RUSH	30	5	8	1	2	1	1	3	2	5	2	2	1	2	2	12
SHERRON COLLINS	22	1	5	0	1	0	0	0	0	0	5	3	1	1	0	2
RODRICK STEWART	8	1	4	0	1	0	0	1	1	2	1	0	0	0	0	2
JEREMY CASE	2	0	0	0	0	0	0	0	0	0	1	0	0	0	0	0
TYREL REED	2	1	2	0	1	0	0	0	0	0	0	0	0	0	0	2
SASHA KAUN	17	2	3	0	0	4	6	2	3	5	0	3	0	1	0	8
COLE ALDRICH	6	0	3	0	0	0	0	2	0	2	0	0	0	0	2	0
MATT KLEINMANN	1	0	0	0	0	0	0	0	0	0	0	1	0	0	0	0
CONNER TEAHAN	0	0	0	0	0	0	0	0	0	0	0	0	0	0	0	0
BRENNAN BECHARD	0	0	0	0	0	0	0	0	0	0	0	0	0	0	0	0
CHASE BUFORD	0	0	0	0	0	0	0	0	0	0	0	0	0	0	0	0
BRAD WITHERSPOON	0	0	0	0	0	0	0	0	0	0	0	0	0	0	0	0
TEAM	0	0	0	0	0	0	0	3	3	6	0	0	0	1	0	0
TEAM TOTALS	200	33	62	4	11	15	19	16	23	39	22	18	10	10	7	85
PERCENTAGES		FG: 53.2%			3PT: 36.4%			FT: 78.9%								

PLAYER	MIN	FG	FGA	3P	3PA	FT	FTA	OR	DR	TOT	A	PF	ST	TO	BL	PTS
TYLER ROCHE	20	0	2	0	2	0	0	1	1	2	0	1	0	1	1	0
SHAMARI SPEARS	29	3	7	0	0	0	0	1	4	5	3	4	0	2	0	6
TYRELLE BLAIR	27	0	2	0	0	1	2	2	3	5	1	2	0	1	5	1
TYRESE RICE	30	6	16	4	9	4	5	0	2	2	1	4	2	6	1	20
RAKIM SANDERS	34	8	15	3	7	2	6	2	1	3	5	1	1	2	0	21
BIKO PARIS	17	1	2	0	0	1	2	0	1	1	0	0	0	2	0	3
COREY RAJI	19	0	4	0	1	1	2	1	0	1	1	2	0	0	0	1
JOHN OATES	23	4	4	0	0	0	0	1	1	2	3	3	0	0	1	8
JOSH SOUTHERN	1	0	0	0	0	0	0	0	0	0	0	0	0	0	0	0
TEAM	0	0	0	0	0	0	0	3	0	3	0	0	0	0	0	0
TEAM TOTALS	200	22	52	7	19	9	17	11	13	24	14	17	3	14	8	60
PERCENTAGES		FG: 42.3%			3PT: 36.8%			FT: 52.9%								

TEAM	1	2	SCORE
LOYOLA-MARYLAND	24	36	60
KANSAS	41	49	90

DATE: 1/8/2008 LOCATION: ALLEN FIELD HOUSE

PLAYER	MIN	FG	FGA	3P	3PA	FT	FTA	OR	DR	TOT	A	PF	ST	TO	BL	PTS
DARRELL ARTHUR	22	5	11	0	1	4	7	2	3	5	0	3	1	0	3	14
DARNELL JACKSON	21	3	6	0	0	3	4	3	6	9	2	2	1	2	1	9
RUSSELL ROBINSON	27	1	3	0	2	3	4	0	2	2	3	2	1	3	1	5
SHERRON COLLINS	28	7	13	3	8	1	3	0	2	2	2	0	3	1	1	18
BRANDON RUSH	24	3	7	0	1	3	5	2	2	4	3	0	2	1	1	9
CONNER TEAHAN	6	2	3	1	2	0	0	1	1	2	0	0	0	1	0	5
RODRICK STEWART	18	1	2	0	1	0	0	2	1	3	2	3	0	0	0	2
JEREMY CASE	12	3	4	2	3	0	0	0	0	0	3	1	2	0	0	8
BRENNAN BECHARD	1	0	0	0	0	1	2	0	0	0	1	0	0	0	0	1
TYREL REED	7	0	1	0	1	0	0	0	0	0	1	0	1	0	0	0
CHASE BUFORD	1	1	2	0	1	0	0	0	0	0	0	0	0	0	0	2
SASHA KAUN	19	4	5	0	0	6	8	2	6	8	0	2	1	2	1	14
BRAD WITHERSPOON	1	0	1	0	0	0	0	1	0	1	0	0	0	1	0	0
COLE ALDRICH	11	1	7	0	0	1	2	3	3	6	1	4	0	1	2	3
MATT KLEINMANN	2	0	0	0	0	0	0	0	1	1	0	1	0	0	0	0
MARIO CHALMERS	0	0	0	0	0	0	0	0	0	0	0	0	0	0	0	0
TEAM	0	0	0	0	0	0	0	2	2	4	0	0	0	0	0	0
TEAM TOTALS	200	31	65	6	20	22	35	18	29	47	18	18	12	12	10	90
PERCENTAGES		FG: 47.7%			3PT: 30%			FT: 62.9%								

PLAYER	MIN	FG	FGA	3P	3PA	FT	FTA	OR	DR	TOT	A	PF	ST	TO	BL	PTS
OMARI ISRAEL	28	2	7	0	0	1	2	0	6	6	0	5	0	2	1	5
MICHAEL TUCK	32	3	12	0	3	2	4	5	4	9	1	4	1	1	0	8
GERALD BROWN	31	4	13	4	9	1	3	4	4	8	0	4	1	8	0	13
BRETT HARVEY	27	1	2	1	2	2	2	0	3	3	4	2	0	3	0	5
MARQUIS SULLIVAN	20	5	13	2	8	0	0	0	1	1	0	3	1	0	1	12
GREG MANNING	11	4	6	1	2	1	1	1	1	2	0	1	2	0	0	10
DAN FICKE	16	0	1	0	0	3	4	2	2	4	1	1	0	0	0	3
JOE MILES	12	0	1	0	0	2	4	0	1	1	2	3	2	3	0	2
BRIAN RUDOLPH	21	1	6	0	1	0	0	1	0	1	3	2	1	2	0	2
GARRETT KELLY	2	0	0	0	0	0	0	0	1	1	1	0	0	0	0	0
TEAM	0	0	0	0	0	0	0	3	2	5	0	0	0	1	0	0
TEAM TOTALS	200	20	61	8	25	12	20	16	25	41	12	25	8	20	2	60
PERCENTAGES		FG: 32.8%			3PT: 32%			FT: 60%								

TEAM	1	2	SCORE
NEBRASKA	30	28	58
KANSAS	42	37	79

DATE: 1/12/2008 LOCATION: LINCOLN, NE

PLAYER	MIN	FG	FGA	3P	3PA	FT	FTA	OR	DR	TOT	A	PF	ST	TO	BL	PTS
DARRELL ARTHUR	20	4	6	0	1	0	0	0	2	2	2	3	0	4	3	8
DARNELL JACKSON	28	3	6	0	0	2	2	1	7	8	0	1	0	0	0	8
RUSSELL ROBINSON	25	4	6	2	4	0	2	1	4	5	3	3	2	2	0	10
MARIO CHALMERS	34	4	9	2	6	4	4	0	2	2	6	1	0	1	0	14
BRANDON RUSH	34	5	11	5	7	4	4	1	5	6	4	0	3	4	1	19
CONNER TEAHAN	1	1	1	0	0	0	0	0	0	0	0	0	0	0	0	2
SHERRON COLLINS	22	2	6	0	3	1	1	0	2	2	2	1	1	3	0	5
RODRICK STEWART	9	0	0	0	0	0	1	1	1	2	1	1	0	0	0	0
JEREMY CASE	2	1	1	1	1	0	0	0	0	0	0	0	0	0	0	3
TYREL REED	2	0	0	0	0	0	0	0	0	0	1	0	1	0	0	0
SASHA KAUN	18	4	6	0	0	2	2	3	0	3	0	4	0	0	1	10
COLE ALDRICH	4	0	0	0	0	0	0	0	3	3	0	2	0	0	1	0
MATT KLEINMANN	1	0	0	0	0	0	0	0	0	0	0	0	0	0	0	0
BRENNAN BECHARD	0	0	0	0	0	0	0	0	0	0	0	0	0	0	0	0
CHASE BUFORD	0	0	0	0	0	0	0	0	0	0	0	0	0	0	0	0
BRAD WITHERSPOON	0	0	0	0	0	0	0	0	0	0	0	0	0	0	0	0
TEAM	0	0	0	0	0	0	0	2	2	4	0	0	0	0	0	0
TEAM TOTALS	200	28	52	10	22	13	16	9	28	37	19	16	7	14	6	79
PERCENTAGES		FG: 53.8%			3PT: 45.5%			FT: 81.3%								

PLAYER	MIN	FG	FGA	3P	3PA	FT	FTA	OR	DR	TOT	A	PF	ST	TO	BL	PTS
ALEKS MARIC	26	7	12	0	0	5	10	2	2	4	3	3	1	2	0	19
SEK HENRY	27	0	2	0	2	0	0	0	3	3	0	1	0	1	0	0
ADE DAGUNDURO	20	0	6	0	0	0	2	2	2	4	1	3	1	0	0	0
COOKIE MILLER	32	1	6	1	4	2	2	0	4	4	2	1	1	1	0	5
RYAN ANDERSON	31	4	12	3	10	1	3	2	2	4	1	1	0	1	0	12
STEVE HARLEY	18	2	6	0	0	1	1	0	1	1	1	0	1	2	0	5
JAY-R STROWBRIDGE	8	2	2	0	0	0	0	0	0	0	0	1	0	2	0	4
SHANG PING	6	0	0	0	0	0	0	0	0	0	0	1	0	1	0	0
PAUL VELANDER	15	3	3	2	2	0	0	0	0	0	1	2	2	0	0	8
CHRIS BALHAM	10	0	0	0	0	2	2	0	1	1	1	2	0	2	0	2
COLE SALOMON	7	1	1	1	1	0	0	0	0	0	2	0	0	0	0	3
TEAM	0	0	0	0	0	0	0	1	2	3	0	0	0	0	0	0
TEAM TOTALS	200	20	50	7	19	11	20	7	17	24	12	15	6	12	0	58
PERCENTAGES		FG: 40%			3PT: 36.8%			FT: 55%								

TEAM	1	2	SCORE
OKLAHOMA	20	35	55
KANSAS	40	45	85

DATE: 1/14/2008 LOCATION: ALLEN FIELD HOUSE

PLAYER	MIN	FG	FGA	3P	3PA	FT	FTA	OR	DR	TOT	A	PF	ST	TO	BL	PTS
DARRELL ARTHUR	24	5	10	0	0	4	4	5	3	8	1	4	0	3	2	14
DARNELL JACKSON	25	8	10	0	0	1	2	1	7	8	0	3	1	0	0	17
RUSSELL ROBINSON	24	0	2	0	2	4	4	0	3	3	5	3	2	1	0	4
MARIO CHALMERS	28	4	5	1	2	4	4	0	2	2	5	2	3	2	0	13
BRANDON RUSH	31	5	10	4	7	2	2	0	9	9	4	0	2	1	0	16
CONNER TEAHAN	1	0	0	0	0	0	0	0	0	0	1	0	0	0	0	0
SHERRON COLLINS	26	4	10	1	4	0	0	1	1	2	3	1	0	0	0	9
RODRICK STEWART	5	1	1	0	0	0	0	0	0	0	0	0	0	0	0	2
JEREMY CASE	4	0	2	0	1	0	0	1	0	1	0	0	0	0	0	0
TYREL REED	2	0	0	0	0	0	0	0	0	0	0	0	0	0	0	0
SASHA KAUN	17	2	5	0	0	0	0	0	2	2	0	2	1	0	2	4
COLE ALDRICH	13	2	3	0	0	2	2	0	3	3	0	1	0	0	3	6
BRENNAN BECHARD	0	0	0	0	0	0	0	0	0	0	0	0	0	0	0	0
CHASE BUFORD	0	0	0	0	0	0	0	0	0	0	0	0	0	0	0	0
BRAD WITHERSPOON	0	0	0	0	0	0	0	0	0	0	0	0	0	0	0	0
MATT KLEINMANN	0	0	0	0	0	0	0	0	0	0	0	0	0	0	0	0
TEAM	0	0	0	0	0	0	0	1	1	2	0	0	0	0	0	0
TEAM TOTALS	200	31	58	6	16	17	18	9	31	40	19	16	9	7	7	85
PERCENTAGES		FG: 53.4%			3PT: 37.5%			FT: 94.4%								

PLAYER	MIN	FG	FGA	3P	3PA	FT	FTA	OR	DR	TOT	A	PF	ST	TO	BL	PTS
BLAKE GRIFFIN	5	0	2	0	0	0	0	0	1	1	0	0	0	0	0	0
LONGAR LONGAR	38	9	18	0	0	3	4	3	2	5	2	1	0	3	1	21
TONY CROCKER	18	4	11	0	2	2	2	2	1	3	1	4	0	2	0	10
DAVID GODBOLD	35	2	9	2	5	0	0	2	5	7	1	3	1	2	0	6
AUSTIN JOHNSON	27	1	4	0	1	0	0	0	1	1	1	1	1	0	0	2
TONY NEYSMITH	1	0	0	0	0	0	0	0	0	0	0	0	0	0	0	0
OMAR LEARY	23	2	5	2	3	0	0	1	0	1	0	3	1	0	0	6
TAYLOR GRIFFIN	34	2	11	0	4	4	4	4	4	8	2	3	1	0	1	8
CADE DAVIS	15	1	4	0	1	0	0	0	3	3	0	1	0	4	0	2
BEAU GERBER	4	0	0	0	0	0	0	0	0	0	0	0	0	0	0	0
TEAM	0	0	0	0	0	0	0	1	1	2	0	0	0	0	0	0
TEAM TOTALS	200	21	64	4	16	9	10	13	18	31	7	16	4	11	2	55
PERCENTAGES		FG: 32.8%			3PT: 25%			FT: 90%								

TEAM	1	2	SCORE
MISSOURI	36	34	70
KANSAS	38	38	76

DATE: 1/19/2008 LOCATION: COLUMBIA, MO

PLAYER	MIN	FG	FGA	3P	3PA	FT	FTA	OR	DR	TOT	A	PF	ST	TO	BL	PTS
DARRELL ARTHUR	21	3	9	0	0	4	7	1	8	9	0	3	0	1	0	10
DARNELL JACKSON	32	5	7	0	0	3	7	1	8	9	1	4	1	3	0	13
RUSSELL ROBINSON	27	3	7	1	1	1	2	1	4	5	5	1	0	4	1	8
MARIO CHALMERS	31	4	7	2	4	8	11	2	3	5	2	3	3	1	0	18
BRANDON RUSH	33	2	14	0	4	9	14	2	7	9	1	3	0	1	0	13
SHERRON COLLINS	25	3	6	1	3	2	2	0	1	1	3	1	1	2	0	9
RODRICK STEWART	9	0	0	0	0	0	0	2	2	4	0	3	1	1	0	0
JEREMY CASE	1	0	0	0	0	0	0	0	0	0	0	0	0	0	0	0
SASHA KAUN	12	1	3	0	0	1	2	2	1	3	0	4	0	2	0	3
COLE ALDRICH	9	1	2	0	0	0	0	1	3	4	0	0	0	0	0	2
CONNER TEAHAN	0	0	0	0	0	0	0	0	0	0	0	0	0	0	0	0
BRENNAN BECHARD	0	0	0	0	0	0	0	0	0	0	0	0	0	0	0	0
TYREL REED	0	0	0	0	0	0	0	0	0	0	0	0	0	0	0	0
CHASE BUFORD	0	0	0	0	0	0	0	0	0	0	0	0	0	0	0	0
BRAD WITHERSPOON	0	0	0	0	0	0	0	0	0	0	0	0	0	0	0	0
MATT KLEINMANN	0	0	0	0	0	0	0	0	0	0	0	0	0	0	0	0
TEAM	0	0	0	0	0	0	0	2	1	3	0	0	0	0	0	0
TEAM TOTALS	200	22	55	4	12	28	45	14	38	52	12	22	6	15	1	76
PERCENTAGES		FG: 40%			3PT: 33.3%			FT: 62.2%								

PLAYER	MIN	FG	FGA	3P	3PA	FT	FTA	OR	DR	TOT	A	PF	ST	TO	BL	PTS
DEMARRE CARROLL	33	2	11	0	2	1	6	5	7	12	2	3	2	1	1	5
VAIDOTAS VOLKUS	10	4	5	0	0	0	0	1	0	1	2	2	0	1	0	8
STEFHON HANNAH	35	7	20	3	10	6	8	1	3	4	6	4	2	3	0	23
JASON HORTON	29	3	4	1	2	0	2	1	3	4	2	5	0	2	0	7
MATT LAWRENCE	29	2	10	1	9	0	0	0	3	3	0	2	2	0	0	5
KEON LAWRENCE	19	2	4	0	1	0	0	0	4	4	1	1	0	3	1	4
J.T. TILLER	9	1	4	0	2	0	0	1	1	2	1	3	1	0	0	2
LEO LYONS	13	4	7	0	0	2	4	0	3	3	0	5	0	0	0	10
MARSHALL BROWN	12	2	4	0	1	2	2	1	1	2	0	3	0	0	0	6
DARRYL BUTTERFIELD	10	0	2	0	1	0	0	0	2	2	0	2	1	0	0	0
TEAM	0	0	0	0	0	0	0	4	2	6	0	0	0	0	0	0
TEAM TOTALS	199	27	71	5	28	11	22	14	29	43	14	30	8	10	2	70
PERCENTAGES		FG: 38%			3PT: 17.9%			FT: 50%								

TEAM	1	2	SCORE
IOWA STATE	32	27	59
KANSAS	42	41	83

DATE: 1/23/2008 LOCATION: ALLEN FIELD HOUSE

		FG		3P		FT		OR		TOT		PF		TO		PTS
DARRELL ARTHUR	19	8	13	0	0	0	0	0	1	1	0	2	0	2	1	16
DARNELL JACKSON	28	9	14	0	0	3	4	4	7	11	2	2	0	0	1	21
RUSSELL ROBINSON	23	4	5	0	1	3	4	0	3	3	4	0	1	4	0	11
MARIO CHALMERS	30	3	6	2	2	2	2	0	4	4	6	3	1	1	1	10
BRANDON RUSH	30	3	7	3	5	2	2	0	5	5	6	1	1	1	0	11
CONNER TEAHAN	3	0	1	0	0	0	0	0	2	2	0	0	0	0	0	0
SHERRON COLLINS	25	1	8	0	1	0	0	0	1	1	2	2	2	1	0	2
RODRICK STEWART	9	1	1	0	0	0	0	2	2	4	0	0	0	1	0	2
JEREMY CASE	3	0	2	0	1	2	2	0	1	1	0	1	1	0	0	2
TYREL REED	3	0	0	0	0	0	0	0	0	0	1	0	0	0	0	0
SASHA KAUN	17	3	5	0	0	0	2	1	3	4	1	3	1	0	1	6
COLE ALDRICH	8	0	1	0	0	2	2	0	3	3	0	3	0	0	2	2
MATT KLEINMANN	2	0	1	0	0	0	0	0	0	0	0	0	0	0	0	0
BRENNAN BECHARD	0	0	0	0	0	0	0	0	0	0	0	0	0	0	0	0
CHASE BUFORD	0	0	0	0	0	0	0	0	0	0	0	0	0	0	0	0
BRAD WITHERSPOON	0	0	0	0	0	0	0	0	0	0	0	0	0	0	0	0
TEAM	0	0	0	0	0	0	0	4	3	7	0	0	0	0	0	0
TEAM TOTALS	200	32	64	5	10	14	18	11	35	46	22	17	7	10	6	83
PERCENTAGES		FG: 50%			3PT: 50%			FT: 77.8%								

PLAYER	MIN	FG	FGA	3P	3PA	FT	FTA	OR	DR	TOT	A	PF	ST	TO	BL	PTS
RAHSHON CLARK	32	2	5	0	0	1	1	1	0	1	0	2	2	0	0	5
CRAIG BRACKINS	31	5	14	2	7	1	2	2	6	8	1	2	0	2	0	13
JIRI HUBALEK	22	4	10	0	3	0	1	2	6	8	0	3	0	1	0	8
BRYAN PETERSEN	29	1	5	1	4	0	1	1	1	2	3	2	0	2	1	3
WESLEY JOHNSON	36	6	17	3	10	6	6	0	2	2	2	3	1	3	0	21
CHARLES BOOZER	2	0	1	0	1	0	0	0	0	0	0	1	0	0	0	0
CAMERON LEE	3	0	1	0	1	2	2	0	1	1	0	0	0	0	0	2
DIANTE GARRETT	20	0	4	0	1	3	4	0	3	3	1	0	1	2	0	3
ALEX THOMPSON	9	0	1	0	1	2	2	1	2	3	0	2	0	1	0	2
BROCK JACOBSON	2	0	0	0	0	0	0	0	0	0	0	0	0	0	0	0
SEAN HALUSKA	6	0	0	0	0	0	0	0	0	0	0	1	0	0	0	0
CORY JOHNSON	4	1	1	0	0	0	0	1	0	1	0	1	1	0	0	2
MARK CURRIE	2	0	0	0	0	0	0	0	0	0	0	0	0	0	0	0
MIKE SMITH	2	0	2	0	0	0	0	0	1	1	0	0	0	0	0	0
TEAM	0	0	0	0	0	0	0	1	2	3	0	0	0	0	0	0
TEAM TOTALS	200	19	61	6	28	15	19	9	24	33	7	17	5	11	1	59
PERCENTAGES		FG: 31.1%			3PT: 21.4%			FT: 78.9%								

TEAM	1	2	SCORE
NEBRASKA	15	34	49
KANSAS	44	40	84

DATE: 1/26/2008 LOCATION: ALLEN FIELD HOUSE

		FG		3P		FT		OR		TOT		PF		TO		PTS
DARRELL ARTHUR	25	8	13	0	0	2	4	3	4	7	0	3	0	3	1	18
DARNELL JACKSON	22	5	10	0	0	3	7	2	6	8	5	0	1	1	1	13
RUSSELL ROBINSON	22	2	3	2	3	3	4	0	2	2	3	2	4	1	1	9
MARIO CHALMERS	27	1	6	0	1	1	3	0	2	2	7	1	0	0	3	3
BRANDON RUSH	28	6	8	5	7	0	0	0	8	8	1	2	3	5	0	17
CONNER TEAHAN	3	0	2	0	1	0	0	0	0	0	1	0	1	0	0	0
SHERRON COLLINS	17	4	5	2	2	0	0	0	1	1	1	2	1	1	0	10
RODRICK STEWART	13	0	2	0	1	2	2	1	2	3	3	1	0	0	0	2
JEREMY CASE	6	0	2	0	1	0	0	0	0	0	1	1	0	1	0	0
BRENNAN BECHARD	2	1	1	0	0	0	0	0	0	0	0	0	0	0	0	2
TYREL REED	5	0	0	0	0	0	0	0	1	1	2	1	0	1	1	0
CHASE BUFORD	2	0	0	0	0	0	0	0	0	0	1	1	0	0	0	0
SASHA KAUN	15	3	7	0	0	0	1	0	3	3	0	3	3	1	1	6
BRAD WITHERSPOON	2	0	0	0	0	0	0	0	0	0	0	0	0	0	0	0
COLE ALDRICH	9	1	1	0	0	0	0	0	4	4	0	1	1	0	2	2
MATT KLEINMANN	2	1	1	0	0	0	0	0	1	1	0	0	0	0	0	2
TEAM	0	0	0	0	0	0	0	4	2	6	0	0	0	0	0	0
TEAM TOTALS	200	32	61	9	16	11	21	10	36	46	25	18	14	14	10	84
PERCENTAGES		FG: 52.5%			3PT: 56.3%			FT: 52.4%								

PLAYER	MIN	FG	FGA	3P	3PA	FT	FTA	OR	DR	TOT	A	PF	ST	TO	BL	PTS
ALEKS MARIC	21	0	6	0	0	0	2	2	7	9	0	3	0	3	1	0
SEK HENRY	22	2	4	1	2	0	0	2	4	6	0	0	0	0	1	5
STEVE HARLEY	26	6	12	0	0	4	6	1	1	2	1	1	1	1	0	16
COOKIE MILLER	28	3	8	0	1	1	2	0	1	1	3	2	4	4	1	7
RYAN ANDERSON	19	1	9	1	7	0	0	0	3	3	0	2	3	1	0	3
NICK KRENK	1	0	0	0	0	0	0	0	0	0	0	0	0	0	0	0
JAY-R STROWBRIDGE	15	0	4	0	2	0	0	0	0	0	0	1	0	2	0	0
ADE DAGUNDURO	22	2	7	0	0	3	4	1	3	4	1	3	1	3	2	7
SHANG PING	9	1	3	0	0	0	3	2	0	2	0	0	0	1	0	2
PAUL VELANDER	10	1	2	1	2	0	0	0	0	0	0	1	0	0	0	3
CHRIS BALHAM	20	2	4	0	0	2	2	1	7	8	0	4	1	0	0	6
COLE SALOMON	7	0	1	0	1	0	0	0	1	1	0	1	0	1	0	0
TEAM	0	0	0	0	0	0	0	2	1	3	0	0	0	0	0	0
TEAM TOTALS	200	18	60	3	15	10	19	11	28	39	5	18	10	16	5	49
PERCENTAGES		FG: 30%			3PT: 20%			FT: 52.6%								

TEAM	1	2	SCORE
KANSAS STATE	38	46	84
KANSAS	36	39	75

DATE: 1/30/2008 LOCATION: MANHATTAN, KS

PLAYER	MIN	FG	FGA	3P	3PA	FT	FTA	OR	DR	TOT	A	PF	ST	TO	BL	PTS
DARRELL ARTHUR	17	5	12	0	0	2	2	5	2	7	1	4	0	2	3	12
DARNELL JACKSON	30	2	2	0	0	3	4	0	4	4	0	2	0	2	1	7
RUSSELL ROBINSON	26	1	8	0	3	4	4	0	2	2	3	5	2	2	0	6
MARIO CHALMERS	30	5	9	2	4	7	8	0	1	1	2	5	0	3	0	19
BRANDON RUSH	37	6	10	3	7	0	0	0	7	7	4	3	1	2	0	15
SHERRON COLLINS	29	5	11	1	3	1	2	0	0	0	2	3	0	1	0	12
RODRICK STEWART	6	1	1	0	0	0	0	2	0	2	0	0	0	0	0	2
JEREMY CASE	1	0	0	0	0	0	0	0	0	0	0	0	0	0	0	0
TYREL REED	0	0	0	0	0	0	0	0	0	0	0	0	0	0	0	0
SASHA KAUN	20	1	1	0	0	0	0	1	2	3	0	2	0	2	2	2
COLE ALDRICH	4	0	0	0	0	0	0	0	0	0	0	1	0	2	1	0
CONNER TEAHAN	0	0	0	0	0	0	0	0	0	0	0	0	0	0	0	0
BRENNAN BECHARD	0	0	0	0	0	0	0	0	0	0	0	0	0	0	0	0
CHASE BUFORD	0	0	0	0	0	0	0	0	0	0	0	0	0	0	0	0
BRAD WITHERSPOON	0	0	0	0	0	0	0	0	0	0	0	0	0	0	0	0
MATT KLEINMANN	0	0	0	0	0	0	0	0	0	0	0	0	0	0	0	0
TEAM	0	0	0	0	0	0	0	1	3	4	0	0	0	0	0	0
TEAM TOTALS	200	26	54	6	17	17	20	9	21	30	12	25	3	16	7	75
PERCENTAGES	FG: 48.1%			3PT: 35.3%			FT: 85%									

PLAYER	MIN	FG	FGA	3P	3PA	FT	FTA	OR	DR	TOT	A	PF	ST	TO	BL	PTS
BILL WALKER	25	9	18	3	10	1	2	3	2	5	1	3	1	4	0	22
MICHAEL BEASLEY	38	9	18	4	4	3	4	1	5	6	2	1	1	4	1	25
BLAKE YOUNG	27	1	3	1	1	0	0	0	2	2	5	5	0	0	0	3
CLENT STEWART	36	3	5	2	3	3	4	3	2	5	1	2	0	2	0	11
DOMINIQUE SUTTON	26	1	6	0	1	0	0	3	3	6	1	4	2	2	1	2
JACOB PULLEN	28	4	9	2	5	10	10	0	0	0	4	2	0	1	0	20
CHRIS MERRIEWETHER	1	0	0	0	0	1	2	0	0	0	0	0	0	0	0	1
DARREN KENT	18	0	4	0	2	0	2	3	1	4	3	4	0	0	0	0
LUIS COLON	1	0	0	0	0	0	0	0	0	0	0	0	0	0	0	0
TEAM	0	0	0	0	0	0	0	3	3	6	0	0	0	0	0	0
TEAM TOTALS	200	27	63	12	26	18	24	16	18	34	17	21	4	13	2	84
PERCENTAGES	FG: 42.9%			3PT: 46.2%			FT: 75%									

TEAM	1	2	SCORE
COLORADO	30	29	59
KANSAS	30	42	72

DATE: 2/2/2008 LOCATION: BOULDER, CO

PLAYER	MIN	FG	FGA	3P	3PA	FT	FTA	OR	DR	TOT	A	PF	ST	TO	BL	PTS
DARRELL ARTHUR	25	4	8	0	0	1	1	2	2	4	2	4	0	4	2	9
DARNELL JACKSON	30	4	7	0	0	10	10	1	3	4	0	4	0	0	0	18
RUSSELL ROBINSON	33	0	2	0	1	1	2	1	3	4	4	1	0	1	0	1
MARIO CHALMERS	29	3	7	0	1	2	3	0	4	4	6	2	3	1	2	8
BRANDON RUSH	32	5	12	2	6	3	4	2	4	6	0	2	0	2	0	15
SHERRON COLLINS	17	4	4	1	1	0	0	0	0	0	1	1	0	5	0	9
RODRICK STEWART	10	0	0	0	0	0	0	0	3	3	1	1	0	1	0	0
JEREMY CASE	2	0	0	0	0	0	0	0	0	0	0	1	0	0	0	0
SASHA KAUN	21	4	5	0	0	4	5	1	2	3	0	2	0	2	1	12
COLE ALDRICH	1	0	0	0	0	0	0	0	0	0	0	0	0	0	0	0
CONNER TEAHAN	0	0	0	0	0	0	0	0	0	0	0	0	0	0	0	0
BRENNAN BECHARD	0	0	0	0	0	0	0	0	0	0	0	0	0	0	0	0
TYREL REED	0	0	0	0	0	0	0	0	0	0	0	0	0	0	0	0
CHASE BUFORD	0	0	0	0	0	0	0	0	0	0	0	0	0	0	0	0
BRAD WITHERSPOON	0	0	0	0	0	0	0	0	0	0	0	0	0	0	0	0
MATT KLEINMANN	0	0	0	0	0	0	0	0	0	0	0	0	0	0	0	0
TEAM	0	0	0	0	0	0	0	3	3	6	0	0	0	0	0	0
TEAM TOTALS	200	24	45	3	9	21	25	10	24	34	14	18	3	16	5	72
PERCENTAGES	FG: 53.3%			3PT: 33.3%			FT: 84%									

PLAYER	MIN	FG	FGA	3P	3PA	FT	FTA	OR	DR	TOT	A	PF	ST	TO	BL	PTS
MARCUS KING-STOCKTON	27	0	0	0	0	3	5	1	2	3	2	4	0	0	2	3
MARCUS HALL	40	5	9	3	6	0	0	1	2	3	5	1	1	3	0	13
CORY HIGGINS	39	5	10	1	2	0	0	1	1	2	3	3	1	1	0	11
DWIGHT THORNE II	25	2	6	1	2	1	3	1	3	4	2	3	2	3	0	6
RICHARD ROBY	38	8	15	4	6	2	2	1	5	6	1	3	1	3	1	22
JAVON CONEY	2	0	2	0	2	0	0	0	0	0	0	0	0	0	0	0
CALEB PATTERSON	5	0	0	0	0	0	0	0	0	0	0	2	0	0	0	0
LEVI KNUTSON	14	0	6	0	5	0	0	0	0	0	1	0	0	0	0	0
JERMYL JACKSON-WILSON	10	2	2	0	0	0	0	1	0	1	0	4	0	2	0	4
TEAM	0	0	0	0	0	0	0	2	0	2	0	0	0	1	0	0
TEAM TOTALS	200	22	50	9	23	6	10	8	13	21	14	20	5	13	3	59
PERCENTAGES	FG: 44%			3PT: 39.1%			FT: 60%									

TEAM	1	2	SCORE
MISSOURI	33	38	71
KANSAS	45	45	90

DATE: 2/4/2008 LOCATION: ALLEN FIELD HOUSE

PLAYER	MIN	FG	FGA	3P	3PA	FT	FTA	OR	DR	TOT	A	PF	ST	TO	BL	PTS
DARRELL ARTHUR	14	4	9	0	0	5	6	4	2	6	0	3	0	1	0	13
DARNELL JACKSON	28	3	6	0	1	0	0	1	8	9	2	2	0	2	2	6
RUSSELL ROBINSON	28	3	6	1	3	0	0	0	1	1	4	0	1	1	1	7
MARIO CHALMERS	32	4	10	1	5	6	9	0	4	4	6	2	0	1	2	15
BRANDON RUSH	33	7	13	3	7	2	2	2	4	6	1	1	0	2	0	19
CONNER TEAHAN	1	0	0	0	0	0	0	0	0	0	0	0	0	1	0	0
SHERRON COLLINS	24	4	8	2	4	2	2	1	3	4	4	0	1	3	0	12
RODRICK STEWART	12	0	3	0	1	0	0	1	2	3	1	1	1	1	0	0
JEREMY CASE	1	0	0	0	0	0	0	0	0	0	0	0	0	0	0	0
TYREL REED	1	0	0	0	0	0	0	0	0	0	0	0	0	0	0	0
SASHA KAUN	13	5	8	0	0	2	2	4	0	4	0	4	0	0	2	12
COLE ALDRICH	12	1	3	0	0	4	4	4	5	9	0	3	0	2	0	6
MATT KLEINMANN	1	0	0	0	0	0	0	0	0	0	0	0	0	0	0	0
BRENNAN BECHARD	0	0	0	0	0	0	0	0	0	0	0	0	0	0	0	0
CHASE BUFORD	0	0	0	0	0	0	0	0	0	0	0	0	0	0	0	0
BRAD WITHERSPOON	0	0	0	0	0	0	0	0	0	0	0	0	0	0	0	0
TEAM	0	0	0	0	0	0	0	2	0	2	0	0	0	0	0	0
TEAM TOTALS	200	31	66	7	21	21	25	19	29	48	18	16	3	14	7	90
PERCENTAGES		FG: 47%			3PT: 33.3%			FT: 84%								

PLAYER	MIN	FG	FGA	3P	3PA	FT	FTA	OR	DR	TOT	A	PF	ST	TO	BL	PTS
DEMARRE CARROLL	25	5	10	0	0	3	6	0	3	3	1	3	0	1	0	13
VAIDOTAS VOLKUS	11	2	3	0	0	2	2	0	1	1	0	5	0	0	1	6
KEON LAWRENCE	36	10	13	0	2	5	7	1	3	4	6	2	1	1	0	25
J.T. TILLER	29	6	12	0	2	1	2	0	2	2	2	4	1	1	0	13
MATT LAWRENCE	34	0	6	0	5	1	2	1	4	5	1	1	2	0	1	1
LEO LYONS	23	5	10	0	1	3	6	1	1	2	1	0	1	1	1	13
JASON HORTON	8	0	1	0	0	0	0	0	0	0	1	0	1	0	0	0
MICHAEL ANDERSON JR.	6	0	0	0	0	0	0	0	1	1	0	0	0	0	0	0
MARSHALL BROWN	11	0	0	0	0	0	0	0	0	0	1	1	0	2	0	0
JUSTIN SAFFORD	12	0	2	0	0	0	0	2	3	5	1	3	0	1	0	0
DARRYL BUTTERFIELD	5	0	3	0	0	0	0	0	0	0	0	2	0	1	0	0
TEAM	0	0	0	0	0	0	0	2	0	2	0	0	0	0	0	0
TEAM TOTALS	200	28	60	0	10	15	25	7	18	25	14	21	6	8	3	71
PERCENTAGES		FG: 46.7%			3PT: %			FT: 60%								

TEAM	1	2	SCORE
BAYLOR	33	57	90
KANSAS	36	64	100

DATE: 2/9/2008 LOCATION: ALLEN FIELD HOUSE

PLAYER	MIN	FG	FGA	3P	3PA	FT	FTA	OR	DR	TOT	A	PF	ST	TO	BL	PTS
DARRELL ARTHUR	33	8	14	0	1	7	9	5	5	10	1	2	2	2	3	23
DARNELL JACKSON	18	3	6	0	0	4	4	1	3	4	1	3	0	0	0	10
RUSSELL ROBINSON	31	4	8	0	2	14	15	2	1	3	1	3	1	0	0	22
MARIO CHALMERS	32	4	5	0	0	2	4	0	5	5	7	2	4	3	0	10
BRANDON RUSH	31	4	12	0	4	1	1	1	6	7	3	5	0	1	2	9
SHERRON COLLINS	28	6	10	0	2	5	7	0	2	2	4	0	1	1	0	17
RODRICK STEWART	2	0	0	0	0	1	2	1	0	1	0	0	1	1	0	1
JEREMY CASE	0	0	0	0	0	0	0	0	0	0	0	0	0	0	0	0
SASHA KAUN	18	2	7	0	0	2	4	1	1	2	0	3	0	0	1	6
COLE ALDRICH	7	1	1	0	0	0	0	0	2	2	0	1	0	0	0	2
CONNER TEAHAN	0	0	0	0	0	0	0	0	0	0	0	0	0	0	0	0
BRENNAN BECHARD	0	0	0	0	0	0	0	0	0	0	0	0	0	0	0	0
TYREL REED	0	0	0	0	0	0	0	0	0	0	0	0	0	0	0	0
CHASE BUFORD	0	0	0	0	0	0	0	0	0	0	0	0	0	0	0	0
BRAD WITHERSPOON	0	0	0	0	0	0	0	0	0	0	0	0	0	0	0	0
MATT KLEINMANN	0	0	0	0	0	0	0	0	0	0	0	0	0	0	0	0
TEAM	0	0	0	0	0	0	0	2	1	3	0	0	0	0	0	0
TEAM TOTALS	200	32	63	0	9	36	46	13	26	39	17	19	9	8	6	100
PERCENTAGES		FG: 50.8%			3PT: %			FT: 78.3%								

PLAYER	MIN	FG	FGA	3P	3PA	FT	FTA	OR	DR	TOT	A	PF	ST	TO	BL	PTS
KEVIN ROGERS	29	3	7	0	0	0	0	3	2	5	0	3	0	2	1	6
JOSH LOMERS	11	1	3	0	0	0	0	2	1	3	0	4	0	1	1	2
CURTIS JERRELLS	33	11	21	4	8	4	5	2	3	5	4	4	1	6	0	30
HENRY DUGAT	29	6	13	1	3	2	2	3	2	5	1	4	1	1	0	15
AARON BRUCE	18	2	7	1	5	2	3	0	2	2	1	2	1	2	0	7
MAMADOU DIENE	24	1	2	0	0	1	2	5	5	10	1	2	0	1	3	3
RICHARD HURD	0	0	0	0	0	0	0	0	0	0	0	1	0	0	0	0
LACEDARIUS DUNN	20	7	14	5	10	4	4	1	3	4	0	3	0	0	0	23
MARK SHEPHERD	12	0	1	0	0	0	0	0	0	0	0	3	0	2	2	0
TWEETY CARTER	24	1	4	1	3	1	2	0	1	1	4	4	1	2	0	4
TEAM	0	0	0	0	0	0	0	2	2	4	0	0	0	0	0	0
TEAM TOTALS	200	32	72	12	29	14	18	18	21	39	11	30	4	17	7	90
PERCENTAGES		FG: 44.4%			3PT: 41.4%			FT: 77.8%								

TEAM	1	2	SCORE
TEXAS	38	34	72
KANSAS	42	27	69

DATE: 2/11/2008 LOCATION: AUSTIN, TX

PLAYER	MIN	FG	FGA	3P	3PA	FT	FTA	OR	DR	TOT	A	PF	ST	TO	BL	PTS
DARRELL ARTHUR	28	10	16	0	1	2	2	2	4	6	0	4	0	1	1	22
DARNELL JACKSON	29	5	10	0	0	3	5	1	3	4	0	2	1	2	0	13
RUSSELL ROBINSON	34	1	6	1	3	0	0	0	4	4	2	3	2	2	0	3
MARIO CHALMERS	27	3	10	1	5	6	7	0	1	1	5	4	1	1	1	13
BRANDON RUSH	30	4	9	2	5	0	0	2	1	3	2	4	0	1	1	10
SHERRON COLLINS	26	1	6	0	3	0	0	1	1	2	4	2	0	2	2	2
RODRICK STEWART	3	0	0	0	0	0	0	0	0	0	0	0	0	0	0	0
SASHA KAUN	21	2	4	0	0	0	0	4	3	7	2	3	0	0	1	4
COLE ALDRICH	2	1	1	0	0	0	0	1	0	1	0	2	0	0	0	2
CONNER TEAHAN	0	0	0	0	0	0	0	0	0	0	0	0	0	0	0	0
JEREMY CASE	0	0	0	0	0	0	0	0	0	0	0	0	0	0	0	0
BRENNAN BECHARD	0	0	0	0	0	0	0	0	0	0	0	0	0	0	0	0
TYREL REED	0	0	0	0	0	0	0	0	0	0	0	0	0	0	0	0
CHASE BUFORD	0	0	0	0	0	0	0	0	0	0	0	0	0	0	0	0
BRAD WITHERSPOON	0	0	0	0	0	0	0	0	0	0	0	0	0	0	0	0
MATT KLEINMANN	0	0	0	0	0	0	0	0	0	0	0	0	0	0	0	0
TEAM	0	0	0	0	0	0	0	3	4	7	0	0	0	0	0	0
TEAM TOTALS	200	27	62	4	17	11	14	14	21	35	15	24	4	9	6	69
PERCENTAGES		FG: 43.5%			3PT: 23.5%			FT: 78.6%								

PLAYER	MIN	FG	FGA	3P	3PA	FT	FTA	OR	DR	TOT	A	PF	ST	TO	BL	PTS
DAMION JAMES	23	4	8	2	4	4	4	3	10	13	2	3	0	0	2	14
CONNOR ATCHLEY	29	6	6	4	4	0	0	1	3	4	2	4	0	1	4	16
A.J. ABRAMS	40	5	13	2	8	2	2	1	2	3	0	2	1	1	1	14
D.J. AUGUSTIN	40	1	13	0	2	8	10	0	2	2	5	1	2	1	0	10
JUSTIN MASON	36	3	8	0	2	3	6	5	3	8	2	2	0	0	0	9
GARY JOHNSON	19	2	5	0	0	3	6	1	2	3	1	2	0	4	0	7
ALEXIS WANGMENE	5	0	0	0	0	0	0	0	0	0	0	0	0	0	1	0
DEXTER PITTMAN	4	0	0	0	0	0	0	0	0	0	0	0	0	0	0	0
CLINT CHAPMAN	4	1	1	0	0	0	0	1	0	1	0	1	0	1	0	2
TEAM	0	0	0	0	0	0	0	2	0	2	0	0	0	0	0	0
TEAM TOTALS	200	22	54	8	20	20	28	14	22	36	12	15	3	8	8	72
PERCENTAGES		FG: 40.7%			3PT: 40%			FT: 71.4%								

TEAM	1	2	SCORE
COLORADO	30	29	59
KANSAS	30	42	72

DATE: 2/16/2008 LOCATION: ALLEN FIELD HOUSE

PLAYER	MIN	FG	FGA	3P	3PA	FT	FTA	OR	DR	TOT	A	PF	ST	TO	BL	PTS
DARRELL ARTHUR	21	4	9	0	0	0	0	3	3	6	2	2	0	0	0	8
DARNELL JACKSON	23	5	7	0	0	2	4	1	1	2	1	2	0	0	0	12
RUSSELL ROBINSON	26	1	2	1	2	1	2	2	3	5	5	0	1	1	0	4
MARIO CHALMERS	30	3	5	3	5	4	4	0	3	3	5	3	2	2	2	13
BRANDON RUSH	27	3	9	1	5	0	0	2	5	7	5	1	1	3	2	7
CONNER TEAHAN	3	0	1	0	1	0	0	0	0	0	1	0	0	1	0	0
SHERRON COLLINS	23	2	6	1	3	0	0	1	4	5	3	1	1	3	0	5
RODRICK STEWART	3	0	0	0	0	0	0	0	0	0	0	0	0	1	0	0
JEREMY CASE	2	0	1	0	0	0	0	0	0	0	0	0	0	0	0	0
BRENNAN BECHARD	1	0	0	0	0	0	0	0	0	0	0	0	0	0	0	0
TYREL REED	8	2	3	2	3	0	0	0	1	1	0	3	0	0	0	6
CHASE BUFORD	1	0	0	0	0	0	0	0	0	0	0	0	0	0	0	0
SASHA KAUN	14	3	6	0	0	2	3	0	1	1	0	0	2	1	1	8
BRAD WITHERSPOON	1	0	0	0	0	0	0	0	0	0	0	0	0	0	0	0
COLE ALDRICH	14	2	5	0	0	2	2	0	4	4	0	1	0	0	3	6
MATT KLEINMANN	3	0	0	0	0	0	0	0	0	0	0	0	0	0	0	0
TEAM	0	0	0	0	0	0	0	3	1	4	0	0	0	0	0	0
TEAM TOTALS	200	25	54	8	19	11	15	12	26	38	22	13	7	12	8	69
PERCENTAGES		FG: 46.3%			3PT: 42.1%			FT: 73.3%								

PLAYER	MIN	FG	FGA	3P	3PA	FT	FTA	OR	DR	TOT	A	PF	ST	TO	BL	PTS
MARCUS KING-STOCKTON	23	1	2	0	0	0	0	0	3	3	1	2	1	0	0	2
MARCUS HALL	39	7	12	1	3	0	0	0	6	6	2	3	0	3	0	15
CORY HIGGINS	35	3	6	1	2	2	2	1	4	5	3	2	1	4	0	9
DWIGHT THORNE II	21	0	1	0	1	0	0	0	0	0	2	1	2	1	0	0
RICHARD ROBY	26	1	11	0	3	0	2	1	2	3	0	4	0	2	0	2
XAVIER SILAS	18	1	6	1	2	4	4	2	0	2	0	1	1	1	0	7
JAVON CONEY	5	0	1	0	1	0	0	0	0	0	0	0	0	0	0	0
CALEB PATTERSON	8	0	2	0	2	0	0	0	2	2	0	1	0	1	0	0
LEVI KNUTSON	17	3	4	2	2	0	0	0	1	1	1	0	0	0	0	8
JERMYL JACKSON-WILSON	8	1	3	0	0	0	0	0	1	1	0	2	0	2	1	2
TEAM	0	0	0	0	0	0	0	1	0	1	0	0	0	1	0	0
TEAM TOTALS	200	17	48	5	16	6	8	5	19	24	9	16	5	15	1	45
PERCENTAGES		FG: 35.4%			3PT: 31.3%			FT: 75%								

TEAM	1	2	SCORE
OKLAHOMA STATE	36	25	61
KANSAS	32	28	60

DATE: 2/23/2008 LOCATION: STILLWATER, OK

PLAYER	MIN	FG	FGA	3P	3PA	FT	FTA	OR	DR	TOT	A	PF	ST	TO	BL	PTS
DARRELL ARTHUR	17	1	3	0	0	4	6	0	2	2	0	5	0	3	1	6
DARNELL JACKSON	36	5	6	0	1	6	6	3	7	10	1	2	0	5	0	16
RUSSELL ROBINSON	38	3	8	0	2	3	3	1	2	3	3	2	1	2	0	9
MARIO CHALMERS	25	4	10	1	3	2	2	1	2	3	2	4	1	4	1	11
BRANDON RUSH	32	5	16	1	4	1	1	3	3	6	1	3	1	3	1	12
SHERRON COLLINS	11	0	1	0	1	0	0	0	0	0	0	2	0	0	0	0
RODRICK STEWART	11	0	1	0	0	0	0	0	1	1	0	0	0	0	0	0
JEREMY CASE	3	0	0	0	0	0	0	0	0	0	0	1	0	0	0	0
SASHA KAUN	17	2	3	0	0	0	1	4	1	5	0	4	0	2	0	4
COLE ALDRICH	9	1	1	0	0	0	0	0	3	3	0	1	1	1	0	2
CONNER TEAHAN	0	0	0	0	0	0	0	0	0	0	0	0	0	0	0	0
BRENNAN BECHARD	0	0	0	0	0	0	0	0	0	0	0	0	0	0	0	0
TYREL REED	0	0	0	0	0	0	0	0	0	0	0	0	0	0	0	0
CHASE BUFORD	0	0	0	0	0	0	0	0	0	0	0	0	0	0	0	0
BRAD WITHERSPOON	0	0	0	0	0	0	0	0	0	0	0	0	0	0	0	0
MATT KLEINMANN	0	0	0	0	0	0	0	0	0	0	0	0	0	0	0	0
TEAM	0	0	0	0	0	0	0	0	1	1	0	0	0	1	0	0
TEAM TOTALS	199	21	49	2	11	16	19	12	22	34	7	24	4	21	3	60
PERCENTAGES		FG: 42.9%			3PT: 18.2%			FT: 84.2%								

PLAYER	MIN	FG	FGA	3P	3PA	FT	FTA	OR	DR	TOT	A	PF	ST	TO	BL	PTS
MARCUS DOVE	22	1	4	1	3	2	2	0	0	0	2	4	1	0	1	5
IBRAHIMA THOMAS	22	1	2	0	1	0	0	0	7	7	1	5	1	4	2	2
BYRON EATON	38	4	10	2	3	16	18	0	3	3	4	3	3	5	0	26
OBI MUONELO	35	3	8	3	5	3	4	0	4	4	2	1	1	4	0	12
JAMES ANDERSON	34	3	7	1	3	0	0	2	1	3	0	3	1	3	0	7
TERREL HARRIS	12	1	2	1	2	1	2	0	0	0	0	4	0	0	0	4
TYLER HATCH	5	0	0	0	0	0	0	0	1	1	0	1	0	0	0	0
MARTAVIUS ADAMS	31	2	4	0	0	1	1	1	1	2	0	2	1	1	0	5
NICK SIDORAKIS	1	0	0	0	0	0	0	0	0	0	1	0	0	0	0	0
MARSHALL MOSES	1	0	0	0	0	0	0	0	0	0	0	0	0	0	0	0
TEAM	0	0	0	0	0	0	0	0	1	1	0	0	0	0	0	0
TEAM TOTALS	201	15	37	8	17	23	27	3	18	21	10	23	8	17	3	61
PERCENTAGES		FG: 40.5%			3PT: 47.1%			FT: 85.2%								

TEAM	1	2	SCORE
IOWA STATE	23	41	64
KANSAS	36	39	75

DATE: 2/27/2008 LOCATION: AMES, IA

PLAYER	MIN	FG	FGA	3P	3PA	FT	FTA	OR	DR	TOT	A	PF	ST	TO	BL	PTS
DARRELL ARTHUR	31	9	18	0	0	0	0	5	5	10	2	4	0	2	0	18
MARIO CHALMERS	36	5	8	3	4	2	2	1	3	4	2	2	2	1	0	15
BRANDON RUSH	37	4	10	3	4	4	5	1	2	3	3	1	1	2	1	15
RUSSELL ROBINSON	29	0	4	0	1	5	6	1	9	10	5	2	0	2	0	5
DARNELL JACKSON	29	3	7	0	0	1	2	2	6	8	0	1	0	2	0	7
SASHA KAUN	16	4	5	0	0	0	1	0	2	2	1	3	0	0	3	8
SHERRON COLLINS	18	2	5	1	2	2	2	1	1	2	1	0	1	4	0	7
COLE ALDRICH	4	0	1	0	0	0	0	0	2	2	0	0	0	0	0	0
CONNER TEAHAN	0	0	0	0	0	0	0	0	0	0	0	0	0	0	0	0
RODRICK STEWART	0	0	0	0	0	0	0	0	0	0	0	0	0	0	0	0
JEREMY CASE	0	0	0	0	0	0	0	0	0	0	0	0	0	0	0	0
BRENNAN BECHARD	0	0	0	0	0	0	0	0	0	0	0	0	0	0	0	0
TYREL REED	0	0	0	0	0	0	0	0	0	0	0	0	0	0	0	0
CHASE BUFORD	0	0	0	0	0	0	0	0	0	0	0	0	0	0	0	0
BRAD WITHERSPOON	0	0	0	0	0	0	0	0	0	0	0	0	0	0	0	0
MATT KLEINMANN	0	0	0	0	0	0	0	0	0	0	0	0	0	0	0	0
TEAM	0	0	0	0	0	0	0	1	1	2	0	0	0	0	0	0
TEAM TOTALS	200	27	58	7	11	14	18	12	31	43	14	13	4	13	4	75
PERCENTAGES		FG: 46.6%			3PT: 63.6%			FT: 77.8%								

PLAYER	MIN	FG	FGA	3P	3PA	FT	FTA	OR	DR	TOT	A	PF	ST	TO	BL	PTS
RAHSHON CLARK	27	0	4	0	1	3	4	3	6	9	0	1	0	0	1	3
CRAIG BRACKINS	17	2	5	0	0	2	2	0	0	0	0	3	0	2	0	6
BRYAN PETERSEN	24	2	5	1	4	0	0	0	2	2	1	0	0	0	0	5
JIRI HUBALEK	33	6	13	1	1	1	4	4	4	8	2	2	1	2	1	14
WESLEY JOHNSON	36	7	16	5	11	1	2	0	3	3	0	3	3	3	0	20
DIANTE GARRETT	28	2	5	0	0	2	3	0	3	3	6	2	1	0	1	6
ALEX THOMPSON	6	0	3	0	1	0	0	1	0	1	0	0	0	1	0	0
SEAN HALUSKA	26	3	7	1	5	3	3	0	1	1	2	4	0	0	1	10
CORY JOHNSON	3	0	1	0	0	0	0	0	1	1	0	0	0	0	0	0
TEAM	0	0	0	0	0	0	0	0	2	2	0	0	0	0	0	0
TEAM TOTALS	200	22	59	8	23	12	18	8	22	30	11	15	5	8	4	64
PERCENTAGES		FG: 37.3%			3PT: 34.8%			FT: 66.7%								

TEAM	1	2	SCORE
KANSAS STATE	29	45	74
KANSAS	41	47	88

DATE: 3/1/2008 LOCATION: ALLEN FIELD HOUSE

PLAYER	MIN	FG	FGA	3P	3PA	FT	FTA	OR	DR	TOT	A	PF	ST	TO	BL	PTS
DARRELL ARTHUR	23	5	10	0	0	0	0	4	1	5	1	5	1	0	1	10
DARNELL JACKSON	20	5	7	0	0	0	1	3	3	6	2	4	1	2	0	10
RUSSELL ROBINSON	28	4	8	2	4	4	6	0	4	4	5	2	4	4	3	14
MARIO CHALMERS	28	2	8	1	3	1	2	1	2	3	4	1	2	4	0	6
BRANDON RUSH	37	7	16	5	9	2	2	3	1	4	3	2	1	1	0	21
SHERRON COLLINS	29	7	12	3	7	1	2	2	1	3	4	0	4	1	0	18
RODRICK STEWART	9	0	1	0	0	0	0	3	0	3	2	1	1	0	0	0
SASHA KAUN	20	3	7	0	0	3	5	4	3	7	0	3	1	1	1	9
COLE ALDRICH	6	0	2	0	0	0	0	1	1	2	0	2	0	1	0	0
CONNER TEAHAN	0	0	0	0	0	0	0	0	0	0	0	0	0	0	0	0
JEREMY CASE	0	0	0	0	0	0	0	0	0	0	0	0	0	0	0	0
BRENNAN BECHARD	0	0	0	0	0	0	0	0	0	0	0	0	0	0	0	0
TYREL REED	0	0	0	0	0	0	0	0	0	0	0	0	0	0	0	0
CHASE BUFORD	0	0	0	0	0	0	0	0	0	0	0	0	0	0	0	0
BRAD WITHERSPOON	0	0	0	0	0	0	0	0	0	0	0	0	0	0	0	0
MATT KLEINMANN	0	0	0	0	0	0	0	0	0	0	0	0	0	0	0	0
TEAM	0	0	0	0	0	0	0	2	2	4	0	0	0	0	0	0
TEAM TOTALS	200	33	71	11	23	11	18	23	18	41	21	20	15	14	5	88
PERCENTAGES		FG: 46.5%			3PT: 47.8%			FT: 61.1%								

PLAYER	MIN	FG	FGA	3P	3PA	FT	FTA	OR	DR	TOT	A	PF	ST	TO	BL	PTS
ANDRE GILBERT	23	0	4	0	2	0	0	2	2	4	0	1	2	3	0	0
BILL WALKER	19	4	8	0	3	1	1	0	2	2	0	3	0	3	1	9
MICHAEL BEASLEY	31	11	23	4	7	13	16	2	9	11	0	2	1	2	3	39
BLAKE YOUNG	34	2	3	0	0	5	5	4	0	4	2	3	2	2	0	9
CLENT STEWART	32	2	7	0	2	2	2	0	3	3	6	1	2	4	0	6
JACOB PULLEN	11	1	4	1	4	0	0	0	1	1	2	1	1	3	0	3
DOMINIQUE SUTTON	21	1	2	0	1	1	2	2	0	2	0	2	0	1	0	3
CHRIS MERRIEWETHER	1	0	0	0	0	0	0	0	0	0	0	0	0	0	0	0
RON ANDERSON	10	0	0	0	0	0	0	0	1	1	1	1	0	0	0	0
DARREN KENT	17	2	5	1	2	0	0	3	0	3	0	3	0	2	0	5
LUIS COLON	1	0	0	0	0	0	0	0	0	0	0	1	0	0	0	0
TEAM	0	0	0	0	0	0	0	3	0	3	0	0	0	0	0	0
TEAM TOTALS	200	23	56	6	21	22	26	16	18	34	11	18	8	20	4	74
PERCENTAGES		FG: 41.1%			3PT: 28.6%			FT: 84.6%								

TEAM	1	2	SCORE
TEXAS TECH	26	25	51
KANSAS	51	58	109

DATE: 3/3/2008 LOCATION: ALLEN FIELD HOUSE

PLAYER	MIN	FG	FGA	3P	3PA	FT	FTA	OR	DR	TOT	A	PF	ST	TO	BL	PTS
DARNELL JACKSON	18	3	5	0	0	4	4	2	7	9	2	1	1	0	0	10
SASHA KAUN	18	4	5	0	0	2	2	1	3	4	2	1	0	1	3	10
RUSSELL ROBINSON	20	5	5	3	3	2	2	0	2	2	3	1	2	2	0	15
RODRICK STEWART	14	2	3	2	2	0	0	1	2	3	2	1	0	1	0	6
JEREMY CASE	12	3	6	3	6	0	0	0	2	2	2	0	0	0	0	9
DARRELL ARTHUR	19	2	5	0	0	2	4	4	5	9	3	0	0	0	0	6
CONNER TEAHAN	5	1	1	1	1	0	0	0	0	0	0	1	0	1	0	3
SHERRON COLLINS	20	5	8	1	3	2	2	0	0	0	3	2	0	1	0	13
BRENNAN BECHARD	2	1	1	0	0	0	0	0	0	0	0	0	0	0	0	2
TYREL REED	10	1	2	0	0	0	0	1	0	1	3	1	0	1	0	2
MARIO CHALMERS	21	4	6	3	4	0	0	0	2	2	3	2	2	3	0	11
CHASE BUFORD	2	0	0	0	0	0	0	0	0	0	0	0	1	0	1	0
BRANDON RUSH	10	3	10	1	4	0	0	2	2	4	1	2	0	0	2	7
BRAD WITHERSPOON	6	0	1	0	1	2	2	0	1	1	2	0	0	2	0	2
COLE ALDRICH	17	5	8	0	0	1	3	2	9	11	0	0	0	0	1	11
MATT KLEINMANN	6	1	1	0	0	0	0	1	1	2	1	0	0	1	0	2
TEAM	0	0	0	0	0	0	0	1	3	4	0	0	0	0	0	0
TEAM TOTALS	200	40	67	14	24	15	19	15	39	54	27	12	6	13	7	109
PERCENTAGES		FG: 59.7%			3PT: 58.3%			FT: 78.9%								

PLAYER	MIN	FG	FGA	3P	3PA	FT	FTA	OR	DR	TOT	A	PF	ST	TO	BL	PTS
TREVOR COOK	19	0	5	0	3	2	2	1	1	2	1	2	0	1	0	2
DAMIR SULJAGIC	13	0	2	0	0	0	0	0	2	2	0	3	0	0	1	0
MARTIN ZENO	33	7	16	1	2	4	4	2	2	4	1	1	1	2	0	19
ALAN VOSKUIL	28	4	10	0	6	0	1	0	1	1	2	0	1	1	0	8
JOHN ROBERSON	31	4	10	4	8	3	6	0	2	2	2	0	1	2	0	15
ROGDRICK CRAIG	5	0	2	0	2	1	2	0	1	1	1	1	1	1	0	1
D'WALYN ROBERTS	14	1	4	0	0	0	0	0	1	1	0	2	1	1	1	2
TYLER HOFFMEISTER	5	0	0	0	0	0	0	0	0	0	0	1	2	0	0	0
MICHAEL PRINCE	1	0	0	0	0	0	0	0	0	0	0	0	0	1	0	0
MIKE SINGLETARY	11	1	4	0	1	0	0	1	0	1	1	1	0	1	0	2
ESMIR RIZVIC	18	0	3	0	0	0	1	4	2	6	0	1	2	1	0	0
CHARLIE BURGESS	16	0	2	0	1	0	0	0	1	1	1	2	0	0	0	0
RICARDO DE BEM	6	1	4	0	0	0	0	0	0	0	0	0	1	0	1	2
TEAM	0	0	0	0	0	0	0	1	2	3	0	0	0	1	0	0
TEAM TOTALS	200	18	62	5	23	10	16	9	15	24	9	14	10	12	3	51
PERCENTAGES		FG: 29%			3PT: 21.7%			FT: 62.5%								

TEAM	1	2	SCORE
TEXAS A&M	26	29	55
KANSAS	36	36	72

DATE: 3/8/2008 LOCATION: COLLEGE STATION, TX

PLAYER	MIN	FG	FGA	3P	3PA	FT	FTA	OR	DR	TOT	A	PF	ST	TO	BL	PTS
DARRELL ARTHUR	28	8	10	0	0	0	0	1	8	9	1	5	0	3	1	16
RUSSELL ROBINSON	29	5	9	0	3	1	1	1	3	4	4	2	2	1	0	11
MARIO CHALMERS	31	6	11	2	4	2	3	1	3	4	0	3	4	2	1	16
BRANDON RUSH	32	2	9	0	2	6	7	3	1	4	1	3	1	3	0	10
DARNELL JACKSON	18	1	2	0	0	0	0	1	6	7	0	5	0	2	1	2
SHERRON COLLINS	32	4	7	0	2	5	6	0	2	2	7	1	3	0	0	13
RODRICK STEWART	1	0	0	0	0	0	0	0	0	0	0	1	0	0	0	0
CHASE BUFORD	0	0	0	0	0	0	0	0	0	0	0	0	0	0	0	0
SASHA KAUN	15	0	3	0	0	1	2	1	0	1	0	2	1	1	0	1
COLE ALDRICH	14	1	3	0	0	1	4	1	1	2	0	1	0	0	0	3
JEREMY CASE	0	0	0	0	0	0	0	0	0	0	0	0	0	0	0	0
BRENNAN BECHARD	0	0	0	0	0	0	0	0	0	0	0	0	0	0	0	0
TYREL REED	0	0	0	0	0	0	0	0	0	0	0	0	0	0	0	0
CHASE BUFORD	0	0	0	0	0	0	0	0	0	0	0	0	0	0	0	0
BRAD WITHERSPOON	0	0	0	0	0	0	0	0	0	0	0	0	0	0	0	0
MATT KLEINMANN	0	0	0	0	0	0	0	0	0	0	0	0	0	0	0	0
TEAM	0	0	0	0	0	0	0	1	3	4	0	0	0	0	0	0
TEAM TOTALS	200	27	54	2	11	16	23	10	27	37	13	23	11	12	3	72
PERCENTAGES		FG: 50%			3PT: 18.2%			FT: 69.6%								

PLAYER	MIN	FG	FGA	3P	3PA	FT	FTA	OR	DR	TOT	A	PF	ST	TO	BL	PTS
DEANDRE JORDAN	26	1	3	0	0	3	6	2	6	8	1	2	0	1	1	5
DONALD SLOAN	36	4	9	3	6	4	4	0	0	0	2	2	0	3	1	15
DOMINIQUE KIRK	30	4	8	2	5	5	6	1	3	4	4	4	0	0	0	15
JOSH CARTER	32	1	11	1	5	2	2	0	1	1	0	3	0	1	0	5
JOSEPH JONES	26	2	7	0	0	3	4	2	4	6	0	2	0	3	0	7
BRYAN DAVIS	25	1	5	0	0	2	4	0	4	4	1	5	2	5	0	4
DERRICK ROLAND	19	1	3	0	1	0	0	1	4	5	0	1	0	0	0	2
BRYSON GRAHAM	0	0	0	0	0	0	0	0	0	0	0	0	0	0	0	0
B.J. HOLMES	0	0	0	0	0	0	0	0	0	0	0	0	0	0	0	0
SHAWN SCHEPEL	0	0	0	0	0	0	0	0	0	0	0	0	0	0	0	0
BEAU MUHLBACH	5	1	1	0	0	0	0	1	0	1	0	2	0	2	1	2
CHINEMELU ELONU	1	0	0	0	0	0	0	0	0	0	0	0	0	0	0	0
NATHAN WALKUP	0	0	0	0	0	0	0	0	0	0	0	0	0	0	0	0
TEAM	0	0	0	0	0	0	0	2	1	3	0	0	0	0	0	0
TEAM TOTALS	200	15	47	6	17	19	26	9	23	32	8	21	2	15	3	55
PERCENTAGES		FG: 31.9%			3PT: 35.3%			FT: 73.1%								

Nick Krug

Acknowledgements

The staff of the Lawrence Journal-World, 6News, Free State Studios, Mediaphormedia and Sunflower Publishing contributed to the coverage of the 2007-2008 Kansas University men's basketball national championship season, including:

The Lawrence Journal-World:
Dennis Anderson, Mike Belt, Karrey Britt, Kim Callahan, Erin Castaneda, John Collar, George Diepenbrock, Jason Elmquist, Mark Fagan, Ann Gardner, Karl Gehring, Sarah Henning, Jonathan Kealing, Katie Kritikos, Chad Lawhorn, C.J. Lehr, Christy Little, Sophia Maines, Christine Metz, Jon Niccum, Nikki Overfelt, Alexander Parker, Jon Ralston, Robert Riley, Susan Roberts, Terry Rombeck, Benton Smith, Jesse Temple, Caroline Trowbridge and Shanxi Upsdell.

6News:
Andrew Baker, Adam Bowman, Mark Boyle, Heather Brummitt, Jesse Fray, Cody Howard, Steve Jones, Nathan Pettengill, Janet Reid, Kevin Romary, Jennifer Schack, Lindsey Slater, John Weldon, D.J. Whetter and Bill Woody.

Free State Studios:
David Coachman, Tommy Gish, Ryan Jones, Justin Kracht, Ann Niccum, Patrick Rea, Nate Riggs, Josh Robison, Dave Severance and J.P. Wofford.

Mediaphormedia:
Isaac Bell, James Bennett, Rich Cornish, Matt Croydon, Ryan Greene, Rebekah Heacock, Chris Hoffman, Alex Kritikos, Nick Nelson, David Ryan, Ben Spaulding and Ben Turner.

Sunflower Publishing:
Designers: Shelly Kemph, Tamra Rolf
Manager: Bert Hull

We greatly acknowledge the effort of the sports and photography departments.

Sports Department:
Sports Editor: Tom Keegan
Associate Sports Editor: Andrew Hartsock
Assistant Sports Editor: Gary Bedore
Sports Copy Editors and Reporters: Chris Cottrell, Bill Cross, Eric Sorrentino, Matt Tait and Ryan Wood
Columnists: Bill Mayer and Chuck Woodling

Photography Department:
Photo Director: Thad Allender
Chief Photographer: Mike Yoder
Photographers: Richard Gwin, John Henry and Nick Krug
Photo Technicians: Brett Garland and Rachel Seymour